COLUMBANUS

Kate Tristram

Columbanus
THE EARLIEST VOICE OF CHRISTIAN IRELAND

the columba press

First edition, 2010, published by
the columba press
55A Spruce Avenue, Stillorgan Industrial Park,
Blackrock, Co Dublin

Cover by Bill Bolger
Origination by The Columba Press
Printed in Ireland by
Colour Books Ltd, Dublin

ISBN 978 1 85607 686-9

Acknowledgements
I should like to thank in particular Allan Hood of the University of
Edinburgh who first suggested that I might write about Columbanus;
Clare Stancliffe of the University of Durham who discussed much of this
material with me; my friend Lillian Groves who read the whole
manuscript and has encouraged me in many ways; many other friends
for their help and support.

Contents

Introducing Columbanus

The name *Columba* (Latin: a dove) with its various forms such as *Colm*, *Colmán* was popular in early Christian Ireland. The most famous man to bear this name was Columba of Iona, founder of the great monastery there and many of its daughter-houses. This book is not about him, but about another of the same name, now usually called *Columbanus* to distinguish him from the Iona saint. If an Irish name has *-án* at the end it means 'little,' or 'lesser', and the *-us* is a Latin ending. There was nothing little about our Columbanus, as the reader will discover, nor did he call himself little! In his letters he referred to himself as 'Columba', or on one occasions as 'Palumbus', a wood-pigeon.

Columbanus enjoyed his name and surely smiled at the fact that never was any man less like a dove. He was pleased to know his name in the three sacred languages of the Bible: 'I am called Jonah in Hebrew, Peristera in Greek, Columba in Latin.' He was a highly literate man with a mastery of Latin, and although he did not know either Hebrew or Greek he enjoyed using Greek words which had been adopted into the Latin language. It is hardly possible to read his letters without feeling how much he enjoyed his own ability to write.

He was born in Leinster in Ireland, perhaps somewhere about the year 550, and his adventurous life took him across southern Europe to die eventually in 615 in Bobbio in Northern Italy. He was dominating, austere, determined, occasionally gentle. His is the earliest voice of Christian Ireland, and this is his story.

CHAPTER ONE

Sources

The first question, for the study of a man who lived so long ago, must be, 'How is anything known about him?' Fortunately for Columbanus there are excellent sources of two kinds: his own varied and extensive writings, and a *Life* written within 30 years of his death. Both raise their own questions.

Columbanus' Writings
Not all of Columbanus' writings have survived. In addition to his extant works he composed a commentary on the Psalms, wrote a treatise on the method of calculating the date of Easter, and a tract against the Arian heresy. Of course he may have written much more, which he does not happen to mention. He wrote entirely in Latin. He left Ireland (c. 591) a very few years before the first known compositions there in the Irish language, and all his existing works, with the possible exception of one poem, date from his time on the continent of Europe. All these works are available in a scholarly edition, Latin and English translation, edited by G .S. M. Walker.* There is no other complete translation of his writings in English, and all references in this book will be to this edition.

First among his writings are his five letters. Letter One is to Pope Gregory the Great, mainly about the date of Easter. Columbanus hopes the Pope will recognise the rightness of the Irish method of calculating, and will use his influence to get it generally adopted. Letter Two is to a Synod of Gallic Bishops, who had summoned him to appear, probably to answer for his deviations about the date of Easter etc. He declines to go, on the grounds that he would simply get angry if he did, and asks them to leave him and his community in peace. Letter Three is a short, tentative let-

---

* *Sancti Columbani Opera*, edited by G. S. M. Walker, published by the Dublin Institute for Advanced Studies, 1970.

ter to a Pope whose name Columbanus does not know, as there has been a vacancy in the Papacy, but whose friendship he hopes for since he has opponents. Letter Four is a farewell to his own monks when he thought he was about to be forcibly deported back to Ireland. In fact he was saved by prompt and perverse action on the part of the winds and the sea and he returned to his community; but this letter shows a more emotional side in another wise very tough man. Letter Five, to Pope Boniface IV, written after Columbanus arrived in Italy and discovered to his dismay that the church was threatened by both heresy and schism, begs the Pope to act strongly against these, and affirms the orthodoxy and loyalty of the Irish people.

There is also a Letter Six, which has to be treated separately. Unlike the others it is not a real letter, but seems to be more of a sermon or a piece for spiritual reading. It is directed to a young monk in the community and could have been requested by him, as it suggests.

Columbanus wrote two Monastic Rules. Not all Abbots did. At this varied, experimental, exciting period of the development of early monasticism it was not considered essential for every Abbot to provide a written rule for his community. Each monastery was independent, and the Abbot could look upon himself as the living Rule, available to deal with questions as they arose. Columbanus wrote the *Monk's Rule*, dealing with princi- ples, and the *Community rule*, dealing mainly with penalties for failures. The Rules together do not give a complete picture of daily life, and later additions were made.

Columbanus' *Penitential*, not as grim as it sounds, aims to pro- vide practical spiritual help, within a relationship of spiritual friendship, for those who need help, encouragement and spiritual medicine on their journey to God. It is directed to the spiritual guides rather than to their clientele. It suggests appropriate remedies for various sins and failings.

The series of 13 sermons were preached by Columbanus to- wards the end of his life, either in Milan or after he had settled at Bobbio. The sermons, to his own monks, deal with the essential of Christian faith and life as he saw it, and may have been intended as his 'last testament'. They emphasise that life is a road, not at all easy, along which the monks must keep travelling with discipline and determination, but the end of it all, in God's kingdom, is glorious beyond expression.

A number of poems are printed in Walker's edition, which he considered genuine works of Columbanus. Only one of these (*Mundus iste transibit*) has survived the critical attention of scholars. Since Walker's edition, another poem he has not included (*Precamus patrem*) has been identified as likely to be by Columbanus.

All these writings will be considered in more detail later. The list above shows the richness and variety of those works of Columbanus which have survived.

The next questions must be 'Are these writings authentically the work of Columbanus? What is involved in the survival of a document?'

The actual pieces of parchment on which Columbanus wrote have not survived. (Occasionally an original does survive, e.g. the *Lindisfarne Gospels*, but obviously there were reasons for the preservation of such a special book.) So scholars have to deal with copies. If the original author was the founder of monastery the monks who followed him would reverence and copy his works, and an appropriate building in which to keep them would give the best chance of survival. But books did not necessarily stay in the place where they were written; as gifts or purchases they travelled extensively.

So detective work is needed when these manuscripts come into scholars' hands. There will be some material clues about their origin: parchment was not made in the same way everywhere or at all times; the style of the script varied widely through place and time, and some monasteries developed very recognisable scripts of their own. The work may have involved the handwriting of more than one scribe, and frequently later readers will have added to the text corrections, comments and glosses (e.g. translations of words). In an age when space for writing was at a premium the empty margins were tempting, and some marginal additions quite unconnected with the main text were appended (The Irish poem 'I and Pangur Bán my cat' was written alongside a commentary on Virgil in a ninth century text from a monastery in Austria.) Margins could contain comments about the weather, or about the state of fatigue of the scribe. But any of these could give the modern scholar valuable information about the date and place of origin of this particular copy.

The text of the manuscript will be read, transcribed (the reader making his own copy) and perhaps translated. Careful and detailed work will be done on the language of the text, since language grows and develops, and particular words and forms of expression come in and out of use. The language will show not only date and place but also the literary skill of the author.

The scholar will consider whether this is the only known copy of this particular work. If there are others he will do some meticulous comparisons, to see whether his text fits into a 'family', i.e. copies of the same work which have the same characteristics or even make the same mistakes. He will make a list of variants, to judge which is more likely to be the original. He will hope to suggest a date and a place for the work in his hand, compared with other copies of the same writing.

All this detailed and painstaking work is completely necessary before a modern reader can take up a medieval text, whether in the original language or in translation, and be satisfied that (as far as our present knowledge goes) this is what the author wrote. But it is exciting detective work. More discoveries are being made all the time, and who knows what is still concealed in the depths of the archives or the cellar of some monastic community or other treasure house?

But definitely it is work for the specialist. Fortunately, for the works of Columbanus, the questions of authenticity has recently been tackled in a book of scholarly studies on his individual writings, *Columbanus: Studies on the Latin Writings*, ed M. Lapidge. The conclusions will be noted as the writings are discussed.

The 'Life of Columbanus and his disciples'

Hagiography, lives of saints written in the Middle Ages, is very different from modern biography writing. The intentions and methods of a modern biographer are clear and easily appreciated.

He (she) will gather as much material as possible, by contacting living witnesses if any and by consulting written or pictorial recorded material of all kinds. He will carefully sift all this, judging the value of his evidence, seeking to discard or at least neutralise his own prejudices, eventually presenting an account of his subject which will emerge, with the many sides of his life, successes and failures, assessed in as balanced a form as the biographer can achieve.

The purposes of the medieval hagiographer were quite different. If his own life was close in time and space to that of his subject, if he includes material that he has gathered from those who knew his subject and references to what was going on in his wider world, the modern historian may find much that is useful. But he will have to quarry for it, and assess it with care, because to provide it was not the intention of the hagiographer. The medieval writer's subject will be God, and God's activity within the life of the saint. He will emphasise all that shows that his subject was an authentic saint, and this will include miracles, spiritual gifts such as prophecy, second sight, converse with angels etc, as well as his moral goodness and life of austerity and prayer. The hagiographer will be writing within a tradition, shaped by the Bible and earlier saints' lives. So he will emphasise those aspects of the life of his saint which fit into the tradition. He will be free to make his selection, is under no obligation to include everything that may be known, and may have excellent reasons for omissions. Perhaps he has a particular readership in mind, and will present his saint in a way that is acceptable or helpful to them. He will certainly hold up his saint for the admiration of the Christian world. The medieval reader of hagiography understood all this: he was not looking for 'history', he was looking for spiritual food.

Hagiography was an immensely popular form of writing and extremely varied. Some of it was factually useless, but highly entertaining. The modern reader of hagiography should not believe all that he is told, nor should he be shocked if, through other sources, he discovers that the hagiography is 'slanted'. A piece of writing should be judged against the values of its own age and its own intentions, not those of a later period, but always approached critically, with the knowledge that many different purposes could lie behind that writing.

Columbanus was well served by his hagiographer. This was a monk named Jonas who, within two or three years of Columbanus' death (23 November 615) joined the Irish saint's final monastery at Bobbio in north Italy. Jonas was from Susa, and was probably either an Italian or a Frank, since the Franks of Burgundy had recently captured the city of Susa. So Jonas never knew Columbanus personally, though he came into a community which would have been full of memories of the Founder. He was an educated man, and the next two Abbots of Bobbio, Athala who succeeded Columbanus and then Bertulf, employed him as a personal assistant/secretary. Although Jonas' career cannot now be traced in detail he was able to travel extensively, particularly in the Frankish territory to the monasteries there founded or inspired by Columbanus. Eventually the Abbot Bertulf asked him to write the *Life* of Columbanus. The book was written in the next three years, but by that time Bertulf, in 639 or 640, had been succeeded by Bobolenus, named by Jonas in the dedication. This enables the book to be dated fairly exactly.

There are two features of Jonas' work to be mentioned now, but examined in more detail later. First, it is a work in two books, and Columbanus dies at the end of Book I. Usually a saint's *Life* would end with his death, which would be narrated in some detail, and followed only by accounts of miracles worked at the shrine which would authenticate his sainthood: they showed he had indeed got to heaven! But Jonas is brief to the point of being laconic about Columbanus' death, mentions his burial and relics with their 'virtues' (signs of power such as miracles) and passes on to his Book II, which is about the activities of Columbanus's disciples. This unusual structure has attracted a lot of attention.

Secondly, the quite unconnected but very fortunate survival of Columbanus' letters have shown a big omission by Jonas in his story of the Life. Letters I-IV, all written in Francia, show to varying degrees Columbanus' awareness of hostility and Letter II makes it specific: the Gallo-Roman bishops are hostile. Only the friendship offered to the Irish monks by the Frankish kings protected Columbanus, until he finally quarrelled with the royal family also and had to leave Francia. Jonas completely suppresses the opposition of the bishops, and put all the blame for Columbanus' departure on the Queen-grandmother, Brunhild. This will be discussed later, but it is a good example of the freedom of the hagiographer to shape his material as he chose.

Jonas will appear very frequently in this study of Columbanus. His work is an excellent example of this type of writing – indeed it is more useful to the historian than most hagiographies. But that Jonas was something other than a historian needs to be kept in mind.

CHAPTER TWO

Childhood and Youth

Jonas begins his story with what is known as a *topos*, that is, a stock theme. He recounts that the saint's mother, asleep one tempestuous night in her late pregnancy, saw a resplendent sun rise from her body and give light to the world. This experience caused her to give great care to the nurture and education of her child once he was born. A similar example is that of St Hild's mother who, according to Bede, in her pregnant dream found a precious jewel under her garment which blazed with light great enough to 'fill all Britain with its gracious splendour'. The purpose of these stories is to set the scene for a saint whose life will convey the spiritual light of God. It was an understood convention, and few of the original readers would have asked questions about historicity.

Jonas then gives some details of Columbanus' childhood, including his early education in the neighbourhood of his home. This is followed by a dramatic story set in his adolescence. He grew into a good-looking teenager, and some of the local girls began to make eyes at him. Jonas of course blames the girls: they are 'lascivious maidens'. But they were beautiful, and he was tempted. One day, in agony of mind, he found that his feet turned in the direction of a nearby cave, where lived a Christian woman hermit. He told her his trouble. Her reaction was immediate and decisive. 'Flee!' she said. 'Flee that temptation. Don't think you can conquer it. Go!' Terrified and elated Columbanus went home and told his mother he was going. She, poor woman, was so distressed that she even lay down across the threshold to stop him. But he leapt over her prostrate body and went.

How true, in the historical sense, is this story? In it we can certainly see the germ of the man Columbanus would become. But it is possible that this too is a *topos*. Jerome's works were very popular, and in one of his letters, to a certain Heliodorus, Jerome writes:

Should you little nephew hang on your neck pay no regard to him; should your mother with ashes on her hair and garments rent show you the breasts at which she nursed you, heed her not; should your father prostrate himself on the threshold trample him under foot and go your way. With dry eyes fly to the standard of the cross. In such cases cruelty is the only true affection.

Jonas may well have read St Jerome.

Could Jonas, in Italy or Francia, really have known anything about Columbanus' early life in Ireland? The writings of the saint are free from any such reminiscences. However, an intriguing detail suggests that Jonas might have had some exact information. For Jonas would hardly have known anything about the development of the Irish language. Yet, in the next section of the story, where Columbanus studies first with a tutor called Sinell and then enters the monastery at Bangor under Abbot Comgall, Jonas quotes the names in the form 'Sinilis' for Sinell, 'Benechor' for Bangor, and 'Commongellus' for Comgall. These would have been the forms of the names when Columbanus lived in Ireland. But by the time Jonas was actually writing, these forms were out-of-date. A development known as 'syncope' had taken place, which is the shortening of a word by the omission of some of its middle letters or forms, and for these three names the forms were now 'Sinlanus', 'Benchor', and 'Comgillus'. So historians have concluded that Jonas must have had a remarkably accurate Irish source for this, probably a written one, possibly from Columbanus himself or from one of the Irish monks who had travelled with him from Bangor, and they have been inclined to accept the information in Jonas' book. We assume then that Columbanus did leave home, however this was achieved, that he studied for a while with Sinell and then entered Bangor.

Columbanus' Childhood Home
Jonas tells us that Columbanus was born somewhere within the area now called 'Leinster', that is, the south-east quarter of Ireland. He does not give a date for his birth. Some writers have suggested 550, or a few years earlier. This is because the first fairly

firm date we have for him is c. 591, when he left Ireland to go to the continent of Europe, and they have supposed he would be a mature man of 40+ by this time. Some of the manuscripts of Jonas say that he was only 20 when he left, others 30. But even 30 seems impossible, given the degree of learning he had amassed before he went. It is better to accept that his date of birth is not known.

Perhaps the most important political fact about Ireland at this time is that it had never been part of the Roman Empire. The westwards expansion of Rome had stopped at the west coast of Britannia. The other people we call Celtic – the Britons, the Gauls – had absorbed in varying degrees *Romanitas*, the quality of being Roman. But the Irish had never known the tramp of the legions, the building of roads, towns and cities, the Roman language and culture. They knew about Rome, of course. They traded across the Irish Sea with the Roman island of Britannia. But the Irish were never conquered, and were immensely proud of that fact. They had no sense of inferiority to pagan, classical Rome.

Irish society was strictly divided into classes, and everyone had an 'honour-price' on his head: that is, he knew exactly how much his attacker would have to pay to his kindred if he were unlawfully killed. Jonas never mentions Columbanus' father, which would have disclosed his class. He mentions that he had relatives; these would have been his father's kin, probably including all the men who claimed descent in the male line from the same great-grandfather. So clearly Columbanus was not of the lowest class, the slaves. What are the other possibilities?

At the top of the social scale were the royal kindred. These included all the men who could claim, within four generations, to be descended from an actual king. Such men were reckoned capable of claiming the throne, and kings would be chosen from among them. But Ireland was a highly divided country. One historian has suggested that there could have been as many as 150 contemporary kingdoms. Clearly some of these must have been tiny, but there must have been a large number of men claiming to belong to 'royal kindred'.

Under them were the 'lords', whose position depended entirely on how many 'clients' they had. A lord would grant a 'fief' to his client, usually not of land but of a number of cattle, and he would receive an agreed return on this. If he became too impoverished to grant fiefs he would sink in social class.

Below the lord was the prosperous farmer. He would receive from a lord and give back, but it was characteristic of him that he had enough animals to be independent of other farmers. He had enough oxen of his own to do his ploughing, and plenty of farm equipment.

Under him was the farmer on a smaller scale, who would re-ceive animals from a lord and owe services in return, but for ploughing he would need to co-operate with other farmers, as per-haps he would have only one ox, few other beasts, and not much equipment.

Under him were the landless people, who could be employed for casual labour on the farm, but who were at least free.

Then there were the slaves, who had no rights of any kind and belonged to their masters. They were probably born as slaves, or had been acquired by slave-raiding or after battle, or had sold themselves into slavery in order to survive.

Most probably Columbanus belonged somewhere in the upper half of this social scale, perhaps the 'prosperous farmer' class. We are told that his mother was able to arrange for him to have the beginnings of an education in literacy, which implies a certain amount of leisure. Had he been lower class he would have been out all day herding the animals. Another possibility is that his family were clients of a monastery, and that, as part of the agreement, the monks had undertaken the education of the eldest son. Later in life Columbanus seems to have adopted a leading role easily, and to have no qualms about addressing kings and writing to Popes, and perhaps these qualities indicate a certain self-confidence arising out of an assured position.

Whatever his social class, Columbanus was born into a farming community, for the whole of Ireland was a farming community. He would have seen no cities or towns, for these were legacies from the Romans to the people they conquered. Even kings and nobles lived on large farms, though the nobility were not expected to do any manual work and the kings were positively forbidden to do so. So the buildings he saw as a child would mostly have been of a uniform pattern, though varying in size: a wooden farmhouse and other farm buildings enclosed by a circular bank or fence, with a small garden for vegetables and herbs but not flowers, and perhaps small enclosed fields for animals or ploughing.

Cattle farming was the principal type, suitable for climate and countryside, and so Columbanus would have seen black, red, brown and dun cows everywhere, and possibly even the rare and precious whites with red ears. Cattle had many uses: for milk and meat, as oxen to pull the ploughs, for leather goods and, later, for parchment for making books, for objects of horn, and tallow candles from the fat. Living cattle were the coinage of the community and an important means of establishing power. Cattle-raiding was one of the accepted occupations of the upper class, and a newly established king would like to show his power by a successful cattle-raid on a neighbouring kingdom. The greatest Irish epic story centred on a cattle-raid, sparked off by jealousy about bulls and resulting in a major war between major kingdoms, which allowed the mythical hero Cú Chulainn to perform his mythical deeds.

Columbanus in childhood would have seen sheep, valued mainly for their wool, and lots of pigs, especially foraging in the woods. The meat-eating classes loved everything made from the pig: joints, bacon, sausages, even black pudding. Poultry would provide eggs and bees honey, which was the only sweetener available. Beeswax was valued, as it provided superior candles.

Cereals were grown for bread and porridge. (The Irish were famous internationally for their porridge!) Wheat was desirable, but barley was more suitable; oats were for the poor. People grew some herbs and vegetables and gathered nuts from the wild. Beer was made from barley.

This, then, was the environment of which the child Columbanus would have become aware. Obviously the people were very dependent on 'nature': a good year would see everyone reasonably prosperous, but a very hard winter or a very dry summer would bring disaster.

Early Christianity in Ireland

Columbanus grew up among Christians, so where did their Christianity come from? There is no reason to connect it with the mission of St Patrick, who worked mainly in the north and west. Later supporters of Patrick wrote and spoke of him as the principal evangelist of the whole of Ireland, but this has no historical accuracy. The writings of Columbanus do not mention Patrick, but we should not assume from this that he had never heard of him, simply that the occasion did not arise. Instead, Columbanus preserves a tradition that the Christian faith came to his people directly from Rome. He writes this in an appropriate context, for in his fifth letter, addressed to Pope Boniface IV, he affirms his people's loyalty, orthodoxy and gratitude to Rome for having sent the gospel to them. At this point he lets his imagination go, and portrays the gospel as a warrior in a chariot of two steeds (SS Peter and Paul) setting out from Rome, charging over the land, surmounting the waves of the sea, to arrive triumphantly at the east coast of Ireland. Does this preserve the memory of any actual visit of a Christian from Rome? Yes, very probably, almost two centuries earlier, and although Columbanus does not name him he can be named: Palladius.

Palladius is known through a chronicler from Gaul: Prosper of Aquitaine. For the year 431 he writes:

> Palladius, having been ordained by Pope Celestine, is sent, as their first bishop, to the Irish who believe in Christ.

The same Pope had laid down the principle that bishops should be sent only to Christians willing to receive them. This suggests that there were Christians in Ireland before 431, who had requested a bishop. The most likely source of their Christianity is the neighbouring island of Britain, where the Christian faith had taken hold during the period of the Roman Empire. Prosper was in a good position to know the facts: he was friendly with Pope Leo who followed soon after Celestine. It is to be noted that he writes that Palladius was the first bishop of the Irish. How does this fit with the view that St Patrick was the pioneer of Christianity in Ireland? The dates of Patrick's work have been much discussed;

probably he was later than Palladius; in any case he worked in a different part of the country; he was not sent from Rome but from Britain; his position as the first missionary saint of Ireland was given to him by enthusiastic partisans rather than by the facts. In any case Patrick in his writings never claimed to be the first missionary in Ireland, though he did have a strong feeling that he might be the last, owing to the impending End of the World.

This involvement in Irish affairs through the sending of Palladius is the first time western Christianity had initiated a mission beyond the boundaries of the former Roman Empire. Why then this sudden interest in Ireland? There may have been two underlying reasons.

First, there was concern over a heresy called Pelagianism. Pelagius was a British Christian whose adult life was spent on the continent, much of it in Rome. He crossed swords with St Augustine (of Hippo, not Canterbury) on the subject of grace and freewill. Briefly, in the whole question of living the Christian life, Pelagius put the emphasis on the human will, on the human decision to obey God in everything, whereas Augustine emphasised the incapacity and weakness of the human will unless enabled and aided in every way by the grace of God. Pelagius' teaching was eventually condemned by the church, though there were those in the extreme west of Europe who continued to see a good deal of sense in it, and it seems that there was such a group in Britain. Palladius appears on the historical scene for the first time in 429, when he was a deacon in Gaul and very worried by this controversy. He persuaded Pope Celestine to send Germanus, Bishop of Auxerre in Gaul, over to Britain to deal with these heretics, either to persuade them or to force them into exile. Exile had been the penalty the Emperor Honorius had decreed against the Pelagians, back in 418. By that date, however, Britain was no longer part of the Empire and so the Britons were not subject to the Emperor's decrees. Where there was no imperial authority the authority of the church might suffice, since the Britons were Christians. But if Germanus was successful, and so turned Christian opinion in Britain against the Pelagians so that they had to leave, where might they go? The answer appeared to be

Ireland, where there was neither imperial nor ecclesiastical authority, and no central political power either. So it would be a good strategy to station in Ireland a bishop sent directly from Rome, and who better than Palladius, who had already expressed great concern about the heresy?

A second and quite different reason for the western church to engage in missionary work outside the limits of the Empire was that the eastern church was already doing this, and the Bishop of Constantinople had claimed the authority to consecrate missionary bishops, contrary to the prerogative of the Pope in Rome, as he asserted.

But tensions like these were not of concern to the Irish. It is likely that they welcomed Palladius and his companions, since he would not have come alone.

Some historians have assumed that his mission was a failure since there is little mention of him in later sources, except for stories of his expulsion from Ireland and even martyrdom. Such stories were probably invented later to emphasise his failure in contrast to St Patrick's success. It is much more likely that Palladius did have successes, but that these were afterwards transferred to the Patrick saga. This is the kind of thing that happened when ecclesiastical parties sought power. Even the names of three missionaries who later appear as Patrick's companions, Auxilius, Iserninus and Secundinus, were perhaps transferred from Palladius' company, since the evidence is that they all worked in Leinster, as did Palladius.

But maybe the best tribute to Palladius is that, almost two centuries subsequently, Columbanus and his people were Christians and retained a memory of his work.

Columbanus' Early Education

The language which Columbanus would have spoken as a child at home was an early form of Irish, now called 'Goidelic' or 'Q-Celtic', because of the number of words beginning with the 'k' sound. It is the ancestor of modern Gaelic. Its nearest relative, spoken by the Britons and the Picts, was 'Brythonic' or 'P-Celtic'; this is the ancestor of modern Welsh, Cornish and Breton. It seems that, in the sixth century, the two languages were not mutually understood. St Columba of Iona had to use an interpreter when preaching to the Picts.

Since Columbanus was brought up in a Christian environment he would have been aware of Latin from an early age, for even in Ireland Latin was the language of the western church. Whatever his experience of 'going to church' may have been he would have heard Latin at any service he attended. But to him Latin was a second language. This was not the case in other Celtic countries, those which had been part of the Roman Empire. For example in Gaul the native language, Gaulic, had given way to Latin and was virtually extinct by about the third century AD. In Britain Brythonic was by no means threatened with extinction, but it had become the language of the uneducated, and Latin, as the language of the conqueror, was felt to be superior.

The position was different in Ireland. A powerful culture expressed in the Irish language existed before Christianity came. It was non-literate, except for a form of inscriptive writing called ogam, and Christianity brought both books and Latin at the same time. But pre-Christian Ireland had learned professions: religious leaders, lawyers, poets; it had a considerable body of lore passed on by apprenticeship to a master and requiring a lot of learning by heart. Learned men held a high place in society and knowledge was admired.

So the Irish, who were proud that they had not been conquered by Rome, were not at all inclined to admire pagan Rome, and were not disposed to regard their own language as inferior to Latin. Indeed they seized the new skills of reading and writing with enthusiasm, and grappled with the new Latin language with determination, as otherwise the sacred books of their new religion would not have been comprehensible to them. But in a remarkably short time, after they had learned the book-arts from Latin culture, they were writing in their own language, and were the earliest people in Europe to write in their own vernacular. They had only the Latin alphabet with which to make Irish noises; it was difficult, but they found ingenious solutions to the problem. By the year 600 they were writing in Irish, both poetry and prose, alongside continuing to write both poetry and prose in Latin.

Whether the child Columbanus saw any books in his own home is not known, but it seems unlikely. Even if he worked with a private teacher rather than in a monastery school it is more than probable that the first book he saw was a Psalter. Verses from the Psalter were normally used for the young beginner to practise his reading or forming his letters. Wax tablets were known, and were useful for making ephemeral notes or copying letters and words. Books were both expensive and precious, for northwestern Europe had no comparatively cheap and plentiful writing material to match the papyrus of the eastern Mediterranean. So real books required parchment, that is, animal skin.

Parchment could be made from the skin of sheep and goats, but the finest was made from calves, and the very finest from very young calves. It had to be manufactured, first by soaking the skin to remove hair and flesh, then by drying, stretching and smoothing. Different techniques showed in the finished membrane, and experts can, for instance, tell the difference between parchment produced in Britain and Ireland and that produced on the continent. Then to make a book the sheets had to be cut to size, and presumably there were fragments left over which would serve as 'scrap paper'. Well-made parchment is almost indestructible (except by fire), but a finished book would be not only expensive but also very heavy, since all the pages were leather.

So even a famous library, such as Bede's library at Jarrow in the eighth century, would not contain many books by our standards. Yet it is surprising how many were available, and how well books travelled. They were produced, of course, largely in the monasteries, which at this time were the centres of Christian learning and the Christian arts of book-production. A monastery would have its *scriptorium*, for those monks who could write legibly. There the scribes would make several copies of books that had been given or lent; their own library would grow and the extra copies would be useful as presents for other religious houses or for distinguished guests. It is known from Columbanus' own letters, and later from the letters of a traveller like Boniface, how much people craved books, and were quite happy to write and ask for them. But in a monastic school a very large amount of learning by heart resulted in the cheapest and lightest way to carry a library: in one's head.

Learning by heart would have been very familiar to the Irish since their pagan culture had all been passed on from living master to living pupil. Whether Columbanus was aware of this pre-Christian culture, whether he had ever seen a 'druid', whether he had ever listened to a 'bard', or heard of a case involving a 'lawyer' is not known. If so he will have realised that there were native Irish learned professions from pre-Christian days. But, even if he knew of them by direct observation, there is no sign that he appreciated their contribution to society. He does indeed look back, later and from abroad, on heroic Irish Christians he has known. But they were all Christians. He has no occasion to mention any pre-Christian wisdom.

Leaving Leinster

So the teenager Columbanus left home and made his way northwards. No doubt his mind often went back to this anchoress in the cave. She had maintained that, since she left home, she had been faithful to her life of prayer, but, had she been a man, she would have sought a more demanding way: 'potior peregrinatio' is Jonas' phrase for this. She would have left Ireland altogether, and this is what she hopes Columbanus will do.

The phrase potior peregrinatio has attracted detailed study. The word peregrinatio itself may be translated 'pilgrimage', but some scholars suggest it should be kept in Latin for, as practised by the Irish, it was so different from the modern understanding of pilgrimage, which generally involves a journey to a place already regarded as holy and then a return home. That kind of pilgrimage, especially to Rome as the burial place of SS Peter and Paul, was going to be popular a little later. In Ireland, a land of many kingdoms, easy travel over the whole country was available only to professional poets and bards. Most of the Irish never travelled outside their own kingdom, for there among their kindred was their work, all their security, indeed the whole purpose of their lives.

Strangers were sometimes encountered in Ireland. One kind was the fellow-Irishman who had simply moved out of his own kingdom, perhaps to marry. But the other kind was the stranger from overseas who, perhaps as a result of having been shipwrecked or even exiled from his country as a punishment, in the nature of things had no relatives and no property, yet had to be recognised in some way by Irish society. He was known as a *'cú glas'*, a 'grey dog' or 'wolf'.

It is suggested that in Ireland *peregrini* (pilgrims) could be of these two types. To leave one's own part of Ireland, one's family and familiar landscape, and settle elsewhere to live a life of prayer was indeed a genuine peregrination. But to leave Ireland altogether was *potior*: more powerful because a more extreme choice.

What were the religious reasons for either lesser or greater *peregrinatio*? They must be set in the context of a movement of great impetus which was sweeping across the Christian world: the movement to asceticism and to the monastic life which embraced it. Its beginnings were back to New Testament times, when there were already those who sought to follow Christ's example of total self-giving by a life of prayer, self-denial and good works. Such a life need not be outwardly dramatic. The New Testament itself gives hints of groups, often of widows, who, while living quietly in their own homes and communities, joined together in this kind of quest.

During the periods of persecution of the church the ultimate in self-giving was martyrdom, for how can a human show more love to God than by making a total and irrevocable gift of himself? The martyrs therefore were specially honoured as the first Christian saints. But the glorious opportunity of martyrdom came only to a few and the church taught that martyrdom should not be sought deliberately. It is not charity to provoke another man to become a murderer! In any case the persecutions came to an end.

Yet, unless the church was to sink into mediocrity as it grew in popularity, there had to be another way of total self-giving for those Christians who resisted the half-hearted and the second-rate. Some experimented by moving to the outskirts of their town or village and there, as solitaries, seeking a life of poverty and

prayer. The next stage was to move further into complete renunci-
ation of civilisation, into the life of the desert: St Antony is generally thought to have been the pioneer here, and very many followed him. But not all who went to the desert were called to solitude; indeed it was realised that solitude could have its dangers,
especially for beginners. So the earliest communities were formed,
and the desert gave a home to two kinds of ascetics, the *solitaries*
and the *nascent* communities. All these together became the
'desert fathers', and the word 'monk', derived originally from the
word which meant 'alone', came to be applied to both kinds of
desert dwellers.

Initially the deserts in question were those in Egypt, Palestine,
Syria, Asia Minor: the eastern Mediterranean generally. But all
the lands bordering on the Mediterranean shared a common culture: the sea united rather than divided, and the ascetic movement
was bound to make its way westwards, growing and developing
as it did so. One name that must be mentioned is that of John
Cassian, who as a young monk had travelled among the Desert
Fathers and observed their lives. As a mature man Cassian settled
in Marseilles, founded monasteries, and set himself to give this
wisdom of the east to the western world, in two very influential
books, the *Institutes* and the *Conferences*. Not very far away, on the
island of Lérins, grew up a community of monks which proved to
be also a training-ground for bishops, sending them to many
places in Gaul and so spreading the monastic ideal. Further north,
Martin, Bishop of Tours, astonished his contemporaries with the
attempt to live simultaneously the life of an ascetic monk in a little
hut and to minister to a great and sophisticated city. And so the
monastic movement crossed the channel to Britain and then, hot
on the heels of Christianity itself, over to Ireland. There, in
Columbanus' youth, it was still new, but was capturing the imagination and drawing on the fervour of new and fervent Christians.

The Irish concept of *peregrinatio* is best understood within this
ascetic movement. Asceticism was not a negative and unhealthy
desire to torture the body. It was a positive attempt to break down
all barriers between God and the Christian. The first barriers to
break are obviously those of sin and sinful habits. Then there are

possible barriers raised by things which in themselves are good and innocent but in some circumstances get in the way of that which is best. Many will serve God in this way in their own home, or in their own monastery. But for some will come the call of God to leave, to go out, to be utterly available to God for whatever might be his will. These are the *peregrini*.

And so the young Columbanus was drawn into a passionate commitment to this way of being Christian. Perhaps, when he spoke with the anchoress, the seed of the desire to go overseas was sown in his mind. But not yet. There was an apprenticeship to be served first. But, even if he did not realise it, when he left home to go northwards out of his own kingdom his *peregrinatio* had begun.

Further Learning
Columbanus did not become a monk immediately. Instead he went to a renowned tutor, Sinell, who was Abbot of his own monastery on Lough Erne, to pursue Biblical studies with him. Jonas does not tell us in detail how much learning Columbanus had acquired before he left home, though he does say that, when the boy was trying to resist the lascivisous maidens, 'he feared lest, ensnared by the lusts of the world, he should in vain have spent so much labour on grammar, rhetoric, geometry and the holy scriptures'. Certainly these skills would not have been much use in the life of a ordinary married Irish farmer. But perhaps Jonas is claiming too much. Had Columbanus been born into a well-to-do Roman family he would have gone through the stages of, first, basic literacy as a small boy, then, as a young teenager, grammar i.e. the correct use of his own language, then, as a late teenager, rhetoric, the elegant and persuasive use of language. An Irish Christian boy's needs would be different. He would make a slower start, since he would have had to grasp the concept of reading, writing and books, which were not part of his general culture, and he would have had to learn Latin from scratch. Of course he would, in the next stage, need the rules of Latin grammar, but the Bible, not the classics, would have been the text he began to study intensively. He might learn to write Latin not sim-

ply correctly but with a flourish: Columbanus did! But still the
aim and crown of all Christian education was exegesis, the ability
to understand and interpret the scriptures. By the time of Bede in
the eighth century the great Irish monasteries had an international
reputation for the study of the Bible and (Bede writes) not only
young Englishmen (Chad, for example) but also young continentals were travelling to Ireland to get the best training available in
Bible study.

It is likely that Columbanus' considerable intellectual powers
developed while he was with Sinell, and that there he wrote his
first book. It appears that this was a commentary on the Psalms,
and it is not quite clear whether it was actually written down or
simply composed in his head. If ever written it seems not to have
survived. Jonas also says that at this stage Columbanus wrote
some hymns. Hymns had not featured in the earliest traditions of
Christian worship, but there is no doubt that Christian poems
were composed and some of these may be included in the writings of the New Testament. (See, for example, Phil 2:6-11: 1 Tim
3:16.) The introduction of hymns into Christian worship is generally attributed to St Ambrose (c.339-397), the powerful Bishop of
Milan whose teaching contributed to the conversion of St
Augustine. He introduced a particular kind of hymn, short, consisting of four lines, easy to memorise, suitable for offices and
special festivals. These became so popular that, even when others
began to imitate the type, the imitations were called ambrosian.
Another type of hymn is connected with the name of St Hilary of
Poitiers (c.315-c.368). His hymns, and others like them, have been
called 'hymns-as-versified-sermons' because they contain a good
deal of information about the life of Christ and Christian doctrine,
and they were used, when heresy was a problem, to combat it and
present orthodoxy.

By the time of Columbanus' young manhood some of these
hymns from the continent were becoming known in Ireland. It is
likely that they were popular among Christians, for pagan Ireland
had a strong poetic tradition: among the learned professionals the
poets had the work of carrying the historical traditions of the local
people, celebrating any victories they might have, and honouring

the achievements of the reigning king; and the Irish poetry in which they did this was extremely complex and sophisticated. Latin Christian poetry which had similar functions would probably have been congenial to Irish Christians. Also, a very little time later, they began to write Irish Christian poetry, and to celebrate the achievements of a saint was the purpose of some of the earliest of it.

So it is extremely likely that the young Columbanus, as soon as he had any facility in Latin, would try his hand at writing poetry. The question of whether any of his poetry has survived will be considered in the next section.

To Bangor
No exact dates are possible, but after some years, presumably, Columbanus decided to enter a monastery, and chose the comparatively new one at Bangor on Belfast Lough, which was still under the rule of its founding Abbot, Comgall. By a tradition (preserved in Adomnán's *Life of Columba*) Comgall was a pupil and friend of Columba of Iona. He was said also to be an extremely strict Abbot, and Bangor became renowned for the austerity of its Rule. The first verse of an appreciative poem about Bangor, probably from the 7th century, describes its way of life:

> Benchuir bona regula,
> Recta atque divina,
> Stricta, sancta, sedula,
> Summa, iusta ac mira.

Does this even need translation? Bangor was 'bona' to the point of being 'mira', but it did this by being 'stricta', to an unusual degree even for an Irish monastery. Whether Columbanus chose it for this reason we have no way of knowing , but this was the setting for the next stage of his life.

CHAPTER THREE

Columbanus at Bangor

Although we are given no details of Columbanus' life at Bangor we may be certain that he was growing and developing in three ways.

First, he was experiencing the monastic life, living under Rule and in complete obedience to the Abbot, taking part in a demanding round of worship and submitting to physical austerity. No *Rule of Bangor* has survived and it may be that none was ever written, since the will of the Abbot served instead. But later Columbanus, as Abbot of his own monasteries, wrote two monastic *Rules*, and it has been conjectured that in them the spirit and perhaps some of the details of life at Bangor lived on. It may be so, but this has remained conjecture.

Secondly, Columbanus would undoubtedly have been extending his biblical knowledge and, thirdly, he would greatly have increased his competence in the Latin language.

Columbanus' Biblical Knowledge

'A Bible' would most probably have been a shelf-full of books at that time. One-volume Bibles could be made: in the eighth century that very intellectual and wealthy house at Wearmouth-Jarrow, Bede's monastery, made three of them, but then they could not be carried, at least by one man. So most monasteries which were lucky enough to have the whole Bible would have had it in several volumes, and many smaller houses would have had to be content with only a part, such as the psalms and gospels, for example.

But it seems that Bangor did have the whole text, for Columbanus, in his later writings, quotes directly from 43 books and has more veiled allusions to others. It is difficult to avoid the impression that he knew the whole Bible virtually by heart! His favourite gospel for quotation is Matthew, and then Luke and

John roughly equally; he does not quote from Mark at all, but this is not surprising as, at the time, Mark was thought to have been rather poor abbreviator of Matthew (rather than the important first gospel discovered by biblical criticism). From the Old Testament the Book of Psalms is most frequently quoted, as might be expected from its constant use in worship.

For modern scholars his quotations throw light on the problem of the diffusion in the Latin-speaking world of a variety of Latin translations of the original Hebrew of the Old Testament and the original Greek of the New Testament. In the early centuries of the church many such 'unofficial' translations into Latin were made. During Columbanus' life in Ireland many of these earlier attempts, known as the 'Old Latin Versions' were still widespread. Eventually they were replaced by St Jerome's official translation, the *Vulgate*. Columbanus' quotations have been analysed, to discover what texts were available at Bangor, and certainly he uses both the 'Old Latin' and the *Vulgate*. But some are from sources not known to modern scholars, so it is not clear whether he is quoting faithfully or whether he is making his own translation or adapting a known text 'creatively'. Some of his quotations are very short, and others are part-biblical sentences incorporated into his own. At no point does he use the method of piling up quotation upon quotation to drive his message home. He is not submerged in his quotations. He is thinking with and through his Bible, but his own voice dominates. But of his extensive familiarity with the text of the Bible there can be no doubt, and it is likely that he acquired this in Ireland before he left.

But one facility he did not acquire at Bangor was a knowledge of Greek and Latin classical literature. There are indeed a few faint echoes of Virgil in his writings, but these could have come from grammatical studies (Virgil was often quoted as an example of excellent style) or from his reading of the Latin fathers. A few decades ago scholars thought they had evidence, particularly in a poem attributed to Columbanus, that he knew the Greek and Latin classics well. Indeed a kind of 'myth' grew up about early Christian Ireland, that it was the home and guardian of European civilisation at a time when the barbarian invasions were destroying so much of this culture on the continent. But it has now been realised that the poems, especially one which gave this impression by its classical references, were the work of a later writer, perhaps a later Columbanus, who lived on the continent. With that realisation the whole picture of a wonderfully cultured Ireland in the classical sense has disappeared. The pagan classics would have been unlikely to appeal to a monastery like Bangor. The Irish achievement was indeed very great, but it centred on Christian and especially biblical studies.

Columbanus' Mastery of Latin

Since Ireland had never been part of the Roman Empire it had no tradition of Latin culture and no memory of Latin spoken as a living language. Irish Christians were in fact the first Europeans to learn Latin as a completely foreign language. How they did it is not known. Latin grammars existed, of which the best-known was by Donatus, but these grammars were written in Latin for Latin speakers. Probably British Christian teachers were involved in Ireland, teaching both the faith and the language. A British writer who influenced Columbanus considerably was Gildas who, writing at the time of the Anglo-Saxon invasions of Britain, denounced the British leaders of church and state for their failure to live by the Christian gospel. Columbanus mentions Gildas' name twice, but his influence is strong on Columbanus' style, especially in Letter 5 where Columbanus feels that the church in Italy is similarly facing ruin.

Both Gildas and Columbanus wrote 'school Latin', that is, Latin which was grammatically correct and showed considerable mastery in the use of stylistic devices: indeed Columbanus' surviving works, which deal with a variety of recipients and situations, allow him to adapt his style competently to suit his purpose. To his continental contemporaries his Latin would have appeared rather old-fashioned, a little too correct perhaps. But at a time when literary culture was collapsing in Gaul because of the barbarian invasions, Columbanus would have thought that his Latin was superior to that of others. He shows no signs of being modest about it.

A New Discovery: a Hymn by Columbanus?

Recently, in addition to Columbanus' writings after he went abroad, attention has focused on a poem which is probably his, dating from his Bangor period or even before. The poem is of course in Latin, and is known by its opening words, *Precamur Patrem*, 'We pray to the Father'. It has been preserved in a small but very important book known as *The Antiphonary of Bangor*. This is not truly an antiphonary, for that would be simply a collection of antiphons (verses in worship recited alternately by two groups). Rather, this little book is a collection of very varied material for use in worship: hymns, antiphons, prayers etc. It may have been the personal collection of the Abbot or another leading monk. It was put together at the end of the seventh century but clearly, in such a book, some of the material might be much older than the final compilation. The book was found at Bobbio, Columbanus' last monastery. But because it has all the external signs of being an Irish manuscript – Irish type of vellum, Irish script etc; and also because it has material specifically about Bangor and its Abbots – most scholars think it originated in the Irish monastery.

Of course, in such a collection of prayers and hymns, it is not usually possible to suggest either date or authorship for any single item. But the poem/hymn *Precamus Patrem*, which stands third in the *Antiphonary*, attracted the attention of one scholar in particular, Michael Lapidge, for two reasons. First, the very rare word *micrologus* occurs in line 81 of this poem and once in Columbanus' first letter and once again his fifth. This is a word of Greek origin, made up of the Greek words for 'small' and 'word'. Columbanus enjoyed words of Greek origin and employed several of them; indeed he enjoyed unusual words generally and could use them with skill. But he could not read Greek, and it is suggested that he saw the word *micrologus* in translation from Greek in Latin of one of the sermons of a Greek monk, Gregory of Nazianzus, made by a Latin scholar, Rufinus. The word is so rare that this is almost the only place where Columbanus could have found it. In this sermon Gregory used it in a discussion about the fitness of representing the Holy Spirit as a small dove. So it is suggested that Columbanus' attention was attracted by the occurrence of his name (*columba*, a dove) and decided to adopt the word micrologus and use it as a sort of signature tune. In so doing he changed the meaning slightly. Rufinus had used it disdainfully to mean 'a trifler' but Columbanus understood it modestly to mean 'of little speech'. So this word occurs twice in Columanus' letters, once in a hymn from Bangor, once in the writings of Rufinus, and virtually nowhere else in the whole of early Christian Latin writing. This certainly needs explanation.

A second reason for connecting *Precamur Patrem* and Columbanus is that there is a parallel between this hymn and Columbanus' fifth letter, where he explains that God the Son was at the same time incarnate on earth and a Person of the Trinity in heaven. In the Latin originals the wording is extremely close and Lapidge's suggestion is the Columbanus composed the hymn in his youth and its wording recurred to him as he wrote the letter in older age.

Most scholars have been convinced by these two pieces of evidence and have accepted *Precamus Patrem* as a composition by Columbanus in his earlier days before he left Bangor.

This is an exciting discovery because from it we can know something of Columbanus' thinking, of his skill in Latin, of his biblical knowledge and of the worship of the monastery at Bangor at that time. It will be remembered (ch 2) that Jonas believed that Columbanus had written some hymns in his youth, even before he went to Bangor. At this time hymns were being newly introduced in to Irish worship from the continent, and even there they were still a fairly novel element in Christian services. There is nothing improbable in supposing that some of Columbanus' hymns were sung by the monks of Bangor.

Precamur Patrem falls into two sections, best dealt with separately. The first section is very clearly an Easter hymn. It uses the characteristic word of the Easter season, Alleluia, and it deals with the typical Easter themes: beginning in the Old Testament with the exodus defeat of the Egyptians at the Red Sea, then to the victory of Christ over evil in the death and resurrection, presented as the conquest of darkness by light, and then to the rescue of the human race. We are able to compare this part of the hymn with another early medieval Easter hymn of praise known as the *Exsultet*, which is used in many churches today at the Easter Vigil and has the same themes. During this vigil the Christian worshipping community re-lives the experience of victory, applying it to their own lives.

So almost certainly the monks of Bangor would have celebrated their version of the Easter vigil with hymns such as these. If Columbanus wrote this first section of *Precamur Patrem* something of the extent of his biblical knowledge and his skill in using it can be seen. To give just one example, he uses the word *primogenitus*, 'first-born'. By this one word, to someone who knew the New Testament well, at least four ideas about Christ would have been suggested: that at the normal level of human birth he was Mary's first-born son (Lk 2:7), that he pre-existed creation and was its first-born (Col 1:15), that in the resurrection he was the first-born from the dead (Col 1:18) and that in relation to others he was the first-born among many brethren (Rom 8:29). This subtle kind of writing was well suited to the monastic practice of reading slowly and extracting the maximum from every word, but it required considerable facility in the writer.

Section 2 of the hymn is quite different and has no parallel in, for example, the *Exsultet*. It is more like the hymns-as-versified-sermons mentioned in chapter 2. These were usually long and recounted the life of Christ or of one of the saints, or expounded some part of the Christian tradition. It is believed that on the continent these hymns had a definite purpose: they were used in places where heresy, particularly Arianism, was a problem and they presented an orthodox picture of Christ.

But this could not have been Columbanus' motive; there was no Arianism in Ireland and at this stage in his life he had probably never heard of it. This section of the hymn goes through the life of Christ, from his pre-existence in the Trinity, his human birth, his performing many miracles, his condemnation and crucifixion, his resurrection and rescue of the dwellers in the realm of death. Perhaps it owes something to the Irish tradition of 'praise-poems' at the courts of kings. It is certainly quite appropriate for the Easter season: at the feast of the victory of Christ what could be more natural than to recount his wonderful deeds?

The sources for the second part of the poem are, first, the gospels, and here 13 passages from St Matthew are used, 5 from Luke, 2 from John and none from Mark. This is completely in line with the general usage of the church at this time. Matthew had become the dominant gospel, partly because of its 'churchy' flavour, especially the passages claiming primacy for St Peter, partly because it contained the bulk of the material in St Mark. Mark, by contrast, was generally out of favour. Indeed it was thought by many scholars of that time to be nothing but an inferior abridgement of Matthew. Where the writer speaks of the rescue of those already in the realm of the dead it is possible that he is making use of the apocryphal *Gospel of Nicodemus* which contains a dramatic account of the 'harrowing of hell', but we can't be sure that he had this text before him as the story was widely current. One detail, the image of the baby Jesus holding the world in his fist, suggests that he had read two (and so probably more) of Jerome's epistles. Another detail seems to echo a third writer, Caelius Sedulius, who wrote an Easter poem which possibly was being quoted here in the description of the miracle of the water-into-wine.

If Columbanus was indeed the author of this poem there is further tantalising evidence here of the books he may have had available in Bangor. He seems, for the extensive quotations in his writings, to have had access to all the books of the Bible and some of the apocryphal works. At some point, presumably at Bangor, he became fully acquainted with John Cassian's monastic writings and, as already mentioned, the writings of the Briton Gildas were very influential. All this suggests that Bangor was building an extensive library and that study was important there.

Precamus Patrem suggests that Irish Latin poetry had begun to develop differently from either classical or Late Latin poetry elsewhere. Classical and Late Latin poems were what is known as 'metrical', that is, based on the 'length' of syllables. This required knowledge of the rules, but would be especially difficult for anyone who had never heard Latin spoken correctly by a native Latin speaker and so would not know, for example, in which circumstances vowels were long or short. Irish poetry developed its own rules. It began to develop some use of rhyme, not known in classical verse, and to experiment with lines based on counting the number of syllables. Both these forms can be seen in this poem but in ways some scholars have thought 'rough'. So this also suggests that the poem is early in date.

Leaving Bangor

In c.591 Columbanus requested permission from his Abbot, Comgall, to go abroad as a *peregrinus*: the 'greater *peregrinatio*' as the anchoress of his teenage experience had described it. At first permission was refused, and it would have been unthinkable to go without it. God's blessing could not be expected by the disobedient. But repeated requests eventually brought that permission and so, probably in the year 591, Columbanus left Bangor. He left, as Jonas narrates, with 12 companions. The number immediately suggests the twelve apostles and no doubt was chosen in conscious imitation of the gospels. Jonas does not give a list of this twelve, but from time to time names some who were probably among them. In one episode, he mentions three monks said to be 'Scots' (i.e. Irish): Comininus, Eunocus and Equanacus, and one British monk Gurganus; it seems likely that they were of the original company. He recounts the death of a monk, another Columbanus, describing him as 'of the same race and name' as the saint and claiming 'they had left Ireland in the same company'. Also Irish was St Gall, who did not go all the way to Italy with Columbanus, but whose exploits deserved his own *Vita*. A certain Lua is mentioned by Jonas as being with Columbanus on his way to his proposed deportation; also named are Domialis (by Jonas) and Libranus (in Letter 4): they could have been among the 12. But reference to a mysterious bishop Aid, who blessed an altar for Columbanus (Letter 4) is too vague for him to be included, even though he had an Irish name.

This little group sailed from Bangor to Brittany. It has been suggested that they could simply have boarded a merchant ship; such ships certainly sailed between Brittany and Ireland and when, later, it was proposed to deport Columbanus such a ship

would have been used to repatriate him. But it is more likely that
they took their own boat, and Jonas reports that they had 'a
smooth sea and a favourable wind'. By the sixth century the Irish
certainly possessed seagoing 'curachs' with oars, a single mast
and a square sail, perfectly capable of making the journey to
Brittany. If the wind was contrary at any point they would have
had to row, and perhaps they did since, on arrival, according to
Jonas, they needed to rest for a while to recover their strength.

But Columbanus did not aim to stay in Brittany. Perhaps the
life and culture of the Bretons, who were simply Britons who had
migrated across the sea as the Anglo-Saxons advanced at home,
was too familiar to him and he wanted a greater challenge. For
whatever reason, he pressed eastwards and entered the territory
of the Franks. At some point soon afterwards he came to the king's
court (probably Guntram, King of Burgundy). Jonas' impression
was that the king took the initiative in this meeting, having heard
of the holy man; it is very likely that the king saw the advantage of
having a holy man living on his land: the kingdom would benefit
from his prayers. So he welcomed the Irish monks and gave them
their first territory, a place in the Vosges mountains known as
Annegray. Columbanus for his part needed both a place for his
monastery and the king's permission and support. So he settled in
that area and, as interest and recruits grew, he founded two further monasteries in the neighbourhood and remained there for
the next twenty years.

CHAPTER FOUR

Columbanus among the Franks

Background to the Franks

The Franks were one of a number of Germanic peoples who, in the days of the strength of the Roman Empire, had lived north of the imperial frontier. The area now called Belgium, and possibly also along the east bank of the Rhine, was their homeland. Other Germanic groups east of them were the Goths (Visigoths in the west and Ostrogoths in the east), the Burgundians, the Vandals, the Lombards and other smaller groups and, in north Germany, the Anglo-Saxons. As mainly pastoral people, these groups had always required space in which to move their flocks and herds, and they had long been enviously aware of the rich lands of the Empire, though many of them had lived in peaceful contact with the Romans. But the growing weakness of the Empire in the fourth century, combined with pressure from the east when an Asiatic people of renowned ferocity, the Huns, began a movement westwards, led to the breaking of the imperial frontier and the infiltration of the Germanic 'barbarians' into the lands of the Empire. The process was gradual. In no part of the Empire was Roman culture suddenly and totally swept away. Many of the barbarians had the greatest respect for the Roman ability to rule and to organise, and wished simply to share its successes.

The rulers of the Franks at this time were a family known as the Merovingians, after a rather misty ancestry called Merovach, the son apparently of a human mother and a sea-monster! The origins of the Franks as a group are themselves rather misty, once their own tradition that they came from Troy has been discounted – this was probably an attempt to ally themselves with the Romans who also traced their origins back to Troy. The Franks seem to have been a loosely-connected group of tribes. They invaded Gaul later than the Goths and the Burgundians, who were already settled in Gaul in the south-west and the south-east respectively. The first

Frankish successful war-leader, traditionally the founder of their power in Gaul, was Clovis, who died in 511. By the time of his death the Franks were dominant in northern Gaul. But at his death his kingdom was divided among his four sons. This appears to have been Clovis' own decision, and it set a precedent for later divisions of territory as if the kingdom were only a piece of personal property. But it had disastrous consequences, as power-hungry brothers became automatically enemies.

During the sixth century the Franks took over those parts of Gaul which had belonged to the Burgundians (Burgundy) and to the Goths (Aquitaine). By the time Columbanus came into the country in c.591 the Frankish land fell into three parts: Austrasia, Neustria and Burgundy. The King of Austrasia when Columbanus arrived was not Sigibert as Jonas claims – he had died in 575; the king was Childebert, who in 591 was King of Austrasia only, but acquired Burgundy also in c.593 on the death of his brother. The area where Columbanus settled was on the borderland between these two kingdoms. After Childebert's death in 596 one of his sons, Theudebert, took Austrasia, and his other son, Theuderic, took Burgundy. This family, including the powerful grandmother Brunhild, continued to support the Irish monks, and, as long as he had this royal support, Columbanus was undisturbed.

The Franks and the Christian Faith
For most of the barbarians from the north (but not the Franks) one particular problem stood in the way of their comfortable assimilation by their new neighbours. In religion they were Arians. Arianism was a form of the Christian faith, but it was judged to be a heresy by the mainstream church, which now called itself Catholic. Any heresy is a way of thinking about and explaining the Christian faith which the mainstream church discards as inadequate or misleading. Arianism takes its name from a priest called Arius, who died in 336, and who was not in fact a major figure in the early church. His heresy shows Christians wrestling with the questions: who exactly is Jesus? What is his relation to God the Father? The answer to this which became orthodoxy, that is 'Catholic' thinking, asserted that Jesus was the incarnation of God

himself, not another and lesser being; that only the Creator who made the human race could redeem it; that the Creator came himself and assumed human nature in Jesus, to live, die and rise again as both 'truly and really man' and 'truly and really God'. But this was complex thinking, hammered out in the early church at the same time as the doctrine of God as Trinity, with much careful balancing of the evidence.

Not everyone balanced the evidence in the same way. It seemed to Arius, and to others who agreed with him, that Jesus was indeed God's son, but created by God at a point in time in order to fulfil this role. A special Arian phrase was 'there was a time when he was not'. To Arians Jesus was a halfway figure, in some ways nearer to man than to God: for example, his knowledge was limited, not infinite. He could be a model and inspiration to human beings, but no more than that: he could not be Saviour.

In the heartlands of Christianity, the countries of the Roman Empire, Arianism had largely died out by about the year 400 and Catholic thinking was normal among Christians. But Arianism had spread outside the Roman Empire, particularly among the Goths who were the only Germanic people to accept the Christian faith while they were still outside the Empire. They had received the faith principally through their apostle Ulfilas, himself a Goth, born in about 311 and so growing up while the Arian controversy was at its height and while Arianism was still supported by many powerful figures within the Christian Church, especially in its eastern half. So he took Arian Christianity to the Goths, and possibly it seemed to them, and to other barbarians accustomed to a hierarchic society, easier to believe in a Son of God subordinated to his Father than in the co-equal Persons of the Catholic Trinity. From the Goths Arianism spread to the Vandals and to the Lombards, and so it re-emerged as a major problem as these people moved into Catholic lands. Hatred between the two groups could be intense, as was shown, for instance, when the Vandals attacked the Catholic cities of the African Mediterranean shore.

But the Franks chose differently. They were not Christians at all before they entered previously Roman territory. Then they accepted the Christian faith, not in its Arian but in its Catholic form. The occasion is said to have been the decision of their leader, Clovis who, finding himself hard-pressed in battle, appealed to the Christian God and won. He then, with a large number of his followers, accepted Christian baptism. This story may be legendary and is perhaps too close to a similar story about the Emperor Constantine. But the fact is clear, and had two main results. For the Franks it meant that they were not at odds with their new 'hosts' in matters of religion, for the new conquerors had accepted the religion of the conquered, and all the richness of western Latin Catholic culture could be theirs; they could even be accepted into social and religious fellowship with the Gallo Romans. A second result was that in later centuries the popes in Rome could look upon the Franks, by then the major power in Europe, as their allies and could themselves offer support to the Frankish emperors.

So Columbanus was unlikely to have met Arianism while he was living among the Franks. When late in life he arrived in North Italy and settled for time in Milan he did come into contact with it, for it was the faith of the Lombard overlords. According to Jonas he wrote 'an excellent and learned work' against it, but this book has not survived.

The Years of Peace

For approximately twenty years, Columbanus could concentrate on the development of the life of the three monasteries in the Vosges mountains, their relationship with the local people, and his own relationship with the Merovingian royal family. These were not entirely peaceful years for, as described later, he aroused considerable opposition from the local bishops. But he could survive this opposition as long as the rulers were friendly. During these years he developed his particular style of monasticism and, as far as we know, had no desire to leave Francia. But then came the decisive quarrel with the royal family.

Jonas' story makes clear from the beginning that, in his view, the evil genius of the whole episode was the Queen grandmother, Brunhild. She had been married to King Sigibert who was murdered in 575; then kingship passed to their son Childebert II, then in 596 to his two sons: Theudebert, who ruled Austrasia, and Theuderic, who ruled Burgundy. Their grandmother was the power behind the throne. At first the young Theuderic considered himself fortunate in having the holy man Columbanus and his monasteries in his kingdom. Theuderic had a number of concubines but no queen, and Columbanus urged him to be lawfully married. But this advice worried Brunhild, who saw her own influence disappearing in the presence of a young queen. So from that point she sought a quarrel with Columbanus. She was, says Jonas, 'a second Jezebel'. Why Jezebel? The first Jezebel was the wife of Ahab, King of Israel, and according to the accounts in 1 Kings 16:22 and 2 Kings 9 she killed the prophets of the Lord, persecuted Elijah, organised the unjust death of Naboth, and finally died a horrible death. Jonas saw several points of connection here, but perhaps his major point was that Brunhild, like Jezebel, persecuted a man of God.

Jonas was probably right in thinking that Brunhild enjoyed power and influence, and that she realised that her continued enjoyment of these things depended on her grandsons for she had no rights simply as a dowager queen. To Jonas she is 'the wretched woman'. But her earlier life had been full of good works, and she was genuinely religious. She had been a Visigothic princess from Spain, and therefore an Arian, but she converted to the Catholic form of the Christian faith on her marriage to Sigibert. She became an influential church patron and founder of monasteries, but on her husband's death, since she had no inclination to become a nun herself, the only option was to rule through her descendants.

The occasion of the quarrel with Columbanus, writes Jonas, was the day she asked him to bless two of the illegitimate sons of Theuderic. Columbanus reacted angrily as a Christian moralist who could not conceivably bless bastards. At this Brunhild may well have been genuinely taken aback, because Frankish custom considered every child born to the king, male or female, to be royal, irrespective of whether the child's mother was the queen or a slave-girl. She was furious: why should this outsider interfere with their customs? Jonas says that she began to persecute monasteries, which is unlikely in general, but she may have begun to change her mind about the monasteries of Irish foundation. After Columbanus left the court on that fateful day, two miracles supported his moral stance. There was a great cracking noise, which Brunhild ignored. Later, when Columbanus went to the king to protest about restrictions apparently placed on his monks, the king sent a propitiatory meal out to him, he refused it and the whole meal exploded. Relations grew worse still when, incited by Brunhild, the king demanded access to the interior of the monastery and was refused. Again, Frankish custom was probably on the king's side, for, after all, the land was a royal gift.

After that, Jonas' story focuses on the determination of Brunhild and Theuderic to remove Columbanus by sending him to the Breton port of Nantes to take ship back to Ireland. At this point a number of miracles happened in his favour. He was sent first to Besancon, where he managed to get entrance to the prison, preached to those under sentence of death, persuaded them to accept 'penance', removed their chains, opened the locked doors of the church to give them sanctuary inside and then, since after all this no one opposed him, nonchalantly walked away and went back to his monastery. When it was known that he was there a band of soldiers was sent to arrest him, but they could not even see him, though he sat calmly there in the middle of the room, reading. Eventually, in order not to endanger others, he agreed to leave.

According to Jonas, all his monks wished to accompany him but the king allowed only those who were Irish or Breton to go. Various miracles of healing, provision and protection took place during his journey towards Nantes. When, going down the river, they were level with the city of Tours, Columbanus wished to visit the shrine of St Martin; the soldiers who guarded him refused permission, but the boat 'sped, as if winged' into the harbour of Tours of its own accord and he was able to spend a night in prayer at the shrine. On arrival at Nantes apparently the monks who accompanied Columbanus, with their luggage, were put on board a ship bound for Ireland, while he himself was allowed to go to the mouth of the river in his skiff. But when the ship tried to leave the port it was washed on to a sandbank by a huge wave and stuck fast. After three days of frustration the captain decided to disembark Columbanus' companions and their goods. Another large wave then carried the vessel away happily on its journey without them. Columbanus and his monks went home to Luxeuil.

But although he had escaped deportation Columbanus realised that there could be no future for him in the area ruled by the hostile king Theuderic. According to Jonas, while he stayed at Tours on his way to Nantes, he had had a moment of prophetic vision and foresaw that within three years Theuderic's family would be annihilated. For the moment he went to the other third of the Frankish territory, the western kingdom of Neustria, ruled by Chlothar, a cousin of the two brothers, who invited Columbanus to stay. At this point the brothers Theuderic and Theudebert, now at war with each other, each asked for Chlothar's support. Columbanus advised him to stay neutral and prophesied that he would inherit both the other kingdoms within three years. The saint declined the offer of a permanent home in Neustria, and was given an escort to conduct him safely to Austrasia, where Theudebert was friendly to him.

He then chose to go to Bregenz, still within Theudebert's territory and, although not wholly pleased with its situation, settled there for a while. He advised king Theudebert to enter a monastery. This suggestion met amused disbelief: 'the king and his companions laughed; they had never heard of a Merovingian on the throne, who had voluntarily given up everything and become a monk'. Then Columbanus warned that the king would be compelled to do what he would not do voluntarily.

When Columbanus first began to think of Italy as a possible destination is not clear, but his decision was taken when, in the war between the two brothers, Theudebert was captured, forcibly tonsured and enclosed in a monastery, then murdered. Bregenz was now in the possession of his old enemy Theuderic and Theuderic's still powerful grandmother, Brunhild. It was time for Columbanus to go and, although the word came true about Theuderic's death and the uniting of the three Frankish kingdoms under Chlothar, by that time Columbanus had set out on his journey to Italy.

A Note about St Gall

Jonas has just one story about Columbanus' disciple, Gall. Columbanus sent Gall to fish and, using his gift of second sight, told him exactly where to go. But Gall, who seems to have had some independence of mind, went to a different river and caught nothing. When he returned empty-handed Columbanus sent him to the place originally mentioned, and of course there was a bumper catch.

Gall's later life was separate from Columbanus and his immediate disciples, and deserved three attempts to write a hagiography. Unfortunately they are all much later that the saint's lifetime. First, an anonymous monk wrote a *Vita* of Gall which contains a reference to an event in the year 771 and so must be later. Secondly, Wettinus, who died in 824, wrote a *Life* at the request of the Abbot of St Gall, who became Abbot in 816; so Wettinus wrote between these dates. But this writing was judged very unsatisfactory, so the same Abbot asked a noted scholar, Walafrid Strabo, to write a *Life of St Gall*, which he probably completed well before that Abbot's death in 837, and he made much use of the first, anonymous *Life*.

These facts are a reminder that it is possible to have quite a lot of hagiography but very little history. But some interesting material is included, such as that Gall had been a pupil of Columbanus before they left Bangor, and that he was ordained priest in Ireland, which, if his ordination was canonically correct, would mean that he was at least 30 years old at that point. These lives also explain the separation between Columbanus and Gall, narrating that Gall was unwilling to set out from Bregenz on the journey to Italy since he was ill at the time. Columbanus thought he simply wished to stay behind and preach, since he had a facility in languages. So Columbanus, in anger, forbade him to celebrate the Mass during his (Columbanus') lifetime. Gall accepted this, but a few years later called his deacon to prepare for the Mass, since he had had a vision of Columbanus' death; he then sent his deacon to Bobbio to discover the truth. Columbanus in dying had instructed that his staff should be sent to Gall as a sign of reconciliation, and the deacon was able to bring also a letter describing Columbanus' last hours.

It may be that there is fact in this story. It seems to be in keeping with what is known about Columbanus that he would have been angry at Gall's refusal to follow; possibly he expected him to rise from his sickbed and be cured. It was also in keeping with his gentler nature that he should feel affection for his old friend and seek to heal the quarrel at the last.

It is important, though, to note the dating of the written evidence, so long after the life of Gall, and to realise the difference between this and the writing of Jonas, who composed his work within the lifetime of many who had known Columbanus. Even Jonas was writing hagiography and not history, as previously explained, but he was writing about a well-known person, and so had to present that person in a convincing way.

CHAPTER FIVE

The Medicine of Penance

Of the religious state of the country when Columbanus first arrived Jonas is very critical. 'The Christian faith had almost departed from that country. The creed alone remained. But the saving grace of penance and the longing to root out the lusts of the flesh were to be found only in a few.' So, says Jonas, Columbanus preached and people began to come to him, drawn partly by his message and partly by the unusually dedicated life they saw in his company. The number of monks began to increase, and so Columbanus founded another monastery a few miles away at Luxeuil, which was to become his main centre. And still the people came to join him and, when he 'perceived that the people were rushing in from all directions to the remedy of penance' (Jonas) he founded yet a third house at Fontaines. For the next twenty years these three monasteries were the centre of his life and his attention.

'The saving grace of penance.' 'The remedy of penance.' It sounds unattractive: was this really what people came for? In what ways did Columbanus meet their need?

Repentance and the hope of forgiveness had always been there in the life of the church and indeed in the preceding religion of the Jewish people, founded as it was on the twin recognition of the righteousness of God and the moral responsibility of humans. In the Old Testament the system of animal sacrifice provided for small, careless and 'unwitting' sins, though not for serious and deliberate ones, for which genuine repentance might avail. In Christianity the sacrificial system was replaced by Jesus' self-sacrificial death. In baptism the new Christian 'died with Christ' and 'rose' to the new life of union with Christ. All sins committed up to that point were forgiven. But what of sins committed after baptism? By its nature (effecting union with Christ) baptism could not be repeated. The early Christians found they had to balance two requirements. On the one hand, they had to maintain a very high standard of moral living against a hostile, and from their standpoint, very immoral world. On the other hand, they had to witness to a God of forgiveness.

So they evolved a system whereby really serious sins (apostasy, adultery, murder: based on an early decision of the church recorded in Acts 15) which effectively cut the sinner off from the Christian community could be atoned for by a period of public penance, at the conclusion of which the sinner was publicly reconciled to the church. Small sins would be dealt with by the usual prayer life of the Christian. But public penance was extremely demanding. In its developed form, after private confession to the bishop the sinner joined the order of penitents for a specific period. During this time he wore distinctive clothing, stood in a particular place in church, and had to leave before communion. His life included fasting and abstinence from sexual relations with his wife. Even after reconciliation with the church the penitent was under life-long disadvantage, and lived always with the knowledge that penance was available once only. Following any repetition of the sin, the sinner was outside.

Of course the great majority of Christians lived their lives without the need for recourse to this, and for those who did fall into serious sin, at least it left open a door of hope; no one was permanently excluded, after one fall, from the life of the church and the life of heaven. But the system proved to be self-defeating. Indeed, people found a way of defeating it, an answer which in Christian theology was ridiculous, but in practice understandable. People postponed baptism, sometimes even up to their deathbeds. This was theologically ridiculous, because baptism was meant to be the beginning of life in the church, a life of union with Christ nourished by the other sacraments and the fellowship of believers. But it was understandable, because a person who received baptism as he was dying would, with all sins forgiven, go straight to heaven in his baptismal innocence. This involved risk, or course: a person might not have a deathbed, or might not be sufficiently conscious on it to ask for baptism. But for some people at least this risk was more tolerable than public penance.

Of course as the years went by there were church leaders who
saw clearly how unsatisfactory this was: how little concerned it
was with the growth in holiness of the average Christian. But the
church was held by a strong bond of loyalty to the earliest generations. Would it not be an insult to the many martyrs who had
died for the faith if things were made easy for later generations?
Would any relaxation of standards not be a capitulation to the pagans
and their immoral way of life? Things of course had changed since
the days of the martyrs: after the Christian faith became legal
there was no temptation to apostasy, and the serious sin of murder
was generally dealt with by the laws of the state. Sexual sins remained for the attention for the church. The environment had
changed; some church leaders at least saw a pastoral need; but
loyalty to the old system prevailed.

The breakthrough seems to have come when the Irish, basing
their thinking on some earlier British material, worked out an alternative at home in Ireland and then, as *peregrini*, took it to the
continent. A number of factors contributed to this. The Irish had
no background of martyrs to whom they had to be loyal. As far as
we know, although it was not without conflict, the conversation
of Ireland happened without shedding any Irish Christian blood
upon Irish soil. They felt a certain independence from classical
Rome and its Mediterranean world, as they were the first country,
outside the original Roman Empire, to be converted to the
Christian faith. Columbanus himself writes to the Pope that he
would love to come to Rome to visit him and the tombs of Peter
and Paul, but the remains of classical Rome mean nothing. The
Irish owed nothing to Roman legal thinking: pre-Christian
Ireland had a worked out system of law which put an emphasis,
when someone had been wronged, on reconciliation through
payment of compensation and the restoration of honour, rather
than on exacting a punishment. They read carefully the writings
of John Cassian, who emphasised the role of the spiritual doctor
(rather than judge) in dealing with sins.

So their system began in the monasteries where the monks
were encouraged to choose a personal spiritual adviser, to whom
they could confide sins, doubts, worries and temptations, and

whose task was to give not absolution but remedy, spiritual medicine so that spiritual health might be restored. This had great advantages: it was confidential, it could be repeated as often as necessary, and it was advice rather than command. So it became popular and spread outside the monasteries to the lay people. We know about it in detail because such was the demand for spiritual guidance that very experienced monks had to write instructions and helps for less experienced guides. Some of these helps have survived and are known as *Penitentials*.

The *Penitentials* are for the most part lists of sins with appropriate penances. Many of these are very demanding and a few quite bizarre. But among these lists can be discerned some of the principles on which the system worked. The general atmosphere was that of the doctor's surgery, not that of the law-court; the penitent was a sick person to be helped, not a criminal to offer satisfaction. He or she must be treated as an individual: in assessing responsibility the adviser must take note of social class, degree of education, even degree of sobriety! John Cassian's principle, 'contraries are cured by contraries', could be very useful. The penitent must never despair. The Irish were capable of saying in one breath, 'This is a very serious sin' and 'but it can be cured.' They did not believe that any sin which was capable of being named was incapable of being atoned for by penance.

Obviously this method could bring great relief to a Christian who was very sensitive to his own failures and keen to arrive in heaven. It could meet the needs of the ordinary Christian for pastoral care and moral growth in the way public penance never could. So it became popular. Some centuries would elapse before it became a sacrament of the church administered only by priests and obligatory for all Christians (in 1215). But the origins of that sacrament have been seen by many historians to lie in the Irish system.

So Columbanus composed a penitential. This text as it now stands was probably the work of many years and of a growing experience. It is likely that he took with him to the continent material that he collected while still at Bangor, for he wrote within a developing tradition of penitential judgements, and he makes use of earlier material such as some of the decisions of British synods on pastoral matters, and particularly the *Penitential of Vinnian*, who was possibly a British monk. Columbanus' work contains provisions for clerics and lay people, as did Vinnian's, and also for monks, though much of his ordering for monks is contained in his *Communal Rule*, to be discussed later. The fact that Columbanus included penances for non-monastic clergy and for laity suggests that he acted as spiritual adviser for both these groups, possibly beginning this kind of work in Ireland and certainly continuing in Francia, as Jonas mentions. Indeed in his first letter, addressed to Pope Gregory the Great, Columbanus states that he has heard confessions of even some of the bishops. Although he crossed swords with the bishops on other matters, such as the date of Easter, there is no evidence that any of them, or the Pope himself, objected to his penitential practice.

The advice given in his penitential was exacting. It dealt seriously with serious sins. For instance, if a cleric (this term is used for clergy who were not monks) had committed murder he should go into exile (itself a severe penalty) for ten years, be under the care of a supervisor and fast on bread and water. At the end of this time he could return but then had to pay the usual blood-money to the relatives of the man he had killed and if necessary take care of the murdered man's parents as would a son. A layman who committed murder had to go into exile, fasting, for three years, and then return to make satisfaction to the dead man's relatives. In the matter of satisfaction the penitential upheld the normal secular custom.

Or, to take the example of theft. A cleric who has stolen once must restore what he has stolen and do penance on bread and water for one year. If he has stolen frequently (and probably is not in a position to make restitution) the penance lasts three years. A layman who has stolen once must restore what he has taken and do penance on bread and water for 120 days (not necessarily consecutively: three periods of 40 days through the year was normal). If he has stolen frequently (and probably cannot make restitution) the penance is one year and 120 days fasting, alms for the poor and a feast for the priest who is advising him.

A cleric does penance for seven years if, after his ordination, he has sexual relations with his own wife. (This reflects the gradually growing opinion that clergy should be celibate.) Contrast this with the provision that a layman who commits adultery with a neighbour's wife does penance only for three years.

These examples will give the feel of what Columbanus recommended for the more serious sins. Clearly, to him, the moral responsibility of a cleric was much greater than that of a layperson. But he was concerned that laypeople also should aspire to Christian virtues. He took seriously, for example, excess in both food and (alcoholic) drink: the penance was one week on bread and water.

To perform these penances, even the smaller ones, could not have been easy. But the intention was kind; as Columbanus himself writes 'so should spiritual doctors treat with diverse kinds of cures the wounds of souls'. The evidence is that many people accepted it as kindness and availed themselves of it.

Columbanus' *Penitential* contains provision for monks, but these will be discussed in the next chapter, along with his monastic *Rules* which have penitential material also.

Some idea of how this system worked may be gained from a monastery slightly older than those of Columbanus: St Columba's Iona. A fascinating *Vita Columbae* was written by the 9th Abbot, Adomnán. It needs care in use because it is of course hagiography and dates from 100 years after the death of its subject in 597. So some of the details may belong to the community in the intervening years rather than to the lifetime of the saint.

It gives a number of examples of Columba's dealing with penitents who had committed serious sins. We are told of two houses where penitents could live with the monks and under their supervision: the unidentified island of Hinba and the monastery of Mag Luinge on the island of Tiree. These penitents would be those whose penance included a number of years in exile.

It seems that those seeking 'the medicine of penance' from Columba would go to Iona to see him. On one occasion, through his spiritual gifts of insight and prophecy, he knew that a man was approaching who had killed his brother, had sexual relations with his mother, and was not genuinely repentant. He refused to allow this man access to Iona, but from the beach 'sentenced' him to 12 years penitential exile away from Ireland. However, as the saint expected, this man did not keep to these terms; he returned to Ireland and was murdered there. Another story shows a truly penitent man greeted very kindly by Columba and assured of forgiveness even before he is sent to Mag Luinge for his penance.

Possibly the most interesting story is of Libran, who came to Columba on Iona and confessed, among other things, that he had killed a man and been sentenced to death. But a wealthy relative paid compensation to the dead man's family, as Irish law permitted. In gratitude the released man vowed to serve his rescuer, and in fact voluntarily became his slave. After a short time he broke this vow and ran away to become a monk: in fact he ran to Iona. Columba sent him to Mag Luinge for 7 years, as penance for the murder. At the end of that time Columba sent him back to his family, first to offer to buy himself out of his slavery to his relative by the gift of a beautiful sword which Columba gave him, and then to help his brothers look after his aged parents. Fortunately his generous relative, encouraged by his generous wife, freed him without the gift. So he looked after his aged father, who died soon after, then his younger brother kindly offered to take his place in the care of their mother, so that he could be free at last to become a monk. A favourable change in the wind gave him a sea-passage back to Iona; Columba then sent him back to Mag Luinge this time as a monk, and eventually, as an old man he was sent back to Ireland and died at the monastery of Durrow, which had been founded by Columba and was part of his monastic family.

The story is interesting in showing that, in Columba's view, penance did not release someone from the just demands of family and society. Penance healed the moral wounds caused by sin, but the requirements of the law must still be met.

For Columbanus' own practice in dealing with penitents there is little evidence of this kind. Jonas (I 34) includes a story of his entering a prison and preaching there to men condemned to death. On receiving their promise to do penance if they were liberated he released them by miraculously breaking their fetters and sending them into a local church where the locked doors were miraculously opened for them to enter and miraculously closed again in the face of the captors who pursued them, but who did not dare then to oppose the divine will for their freedom.

But Jonas' second book, concerning the lives of Columbanus' disciples after his death, has several examples of the use of penance, especially among the nuns of Faremoutiers, a community strongly influenced by the Columbanian tradition.

A later development, after Columbanus' death as far as we know from the evidence, was that the life of penance came to be seen as a kind of martyrdom. The Irish were already familiar with 'red martyrdom' (dying for Christ) and 'white martyrdom' (a life-long dedication, such as that of the Desert Fathers). But penitential practices were very similar to the ascetic practices of the monks and, as mentioned, some penitents lived out their time of penance in association with monks, sharing their ways of life. The life of penance came to be called 'blue martyrdom'. It was a brilliant move. The penitential system from its origin was based on hope: hope that the gates of heaven would not be finally closed against the penitent. But martyrs were not just allowed into heaven: they were positively welcomed there!

The Delights of the 'Gospel Life'
'The medicine of penance' drew people to the monks and to the spiritual help they could offer. But for people to decide actually to become monks (and Columbanus' monasteries certainly grew) there must have been something else: a vision of the goodness of that way of life and of the life of heaven to which it was leading. Some understanding of the attraction may be gathered from the only poem (apart from *Precamur Patrem*) now held to be authentically by Columbanus. In it he addresses a young man, real or fictional, to draw him and place before him the claims of the Christian i.e. the monastic life. This poem is known by its first words: *Mundus Iste Transibit*, 'that world will pass away'.

The young man has his life before him and his significant choices are yet to be made. Columbanus implores him to see for himself that this world is transitory and all human beings die.

How remarkable then (he says) that so many choose to love and trust the things which they cannot keep, which life daily removes from them. They turn their backs on God and choose evil, or at best choose the shallow things which belong to this dark and passing world. But see (urges Columbanus) the outcome of their lives, how short are their pleasures. So reject those temptations and choose the life Christ offers. For the life with God which awaits those who have been faithful to him is extremely lovely. There, beyond death, is the companionship of loving angels and of humans delivered from age, hunger and pain. There is neither death nor suffering. There is celestial food. There is the joy of seeing God, of praising him, or reigning with him. So, young man, see all this and choose bravely.

Of course this not an original message, nor would Columbanus have wanted it to be original. Although there are comparatively few direct biblical quotations in the poems, the biblical message is everywhere. From the beginning the Old Testament cries out that humans can and must choose: choose God, choose obedience, choose life.

But in particular those biblical books known collectively as 'the Wisdom literature', and especially the books of Proverbs and Ecclesiasticus, speak as to an individual young man, calling him 'my son' and urging him to choose between the 'two ways', the way of self-indulgence which leads directly to death, and the way of God, of goodness, which leads to happiness and fulfilment.

This theme of the 'two ways' is again clear in the New Testament, especially in the Sermon on the Mount: 'Enter through the narrow gate; for the gate is wide and the road is easy that leads to destruction, and there are many who take it. For the gate is narrow and the road is hard that leads to life, and there are few who find it' (Mt 7:13-14).

But the New Testament, with its experience of the resurrection of Christ and its forward-looking thrust, goes beyond the Wisdom literature in promising the life of heaven. Columbanus in this poem draws specially on the picture language of the Book of Revelation. It would have seemed to him entirely right to do so: God had deliberately set these beautiful hopes and desires in

front of humans. But heaven does not just happen; it is the consequence of a choice of lifestyle, lived out with love, hope and gen-
erosity and with a clear-eyed knowledge of the alternative.

So Columbanus wrote and so he would have spoken. The message put into a poem would be made memorable. We have no idea
at what point in his life he wrote this poem, but the same message
is there in the piece of writing known as Letter 6, and also in the set
of 13 sermons preached probably in the last year of his life. These
will be considered later.

CHAPTER SIX

In Francia: Life within the Monastery

Columbanus' two Rules, the *Monks' Rule* and the *Communal Rule*, are the principal source of our knowledge of his form of monasticism. They are usually treated separately, as they appear to fulfil different functions in the life of the community. The *Monks' Rule* deals with the principle of the monastic life; the *Communal Rule* contains practical details, with considerable emphasis on maintaining good order and harmony within the common life.

The Monks' Rule

As now printed this consists of ten chapters of varying length. But some of the manuscripts omit chapter 10, which has been recognised as an adapted quotation from Jerome, added to the original Rule at a later date. Others omit chapter 7, which consists of detailed rules for the daily offices, which hardly belongs among the more general themes and will be dealt with later. The *Monks' Rule* gives the fundamentals of the way of life.

The dominant virtue is obedience, and so Columbanus deals with this first. The monk shows his willingness by immediately standing up 'at the first word of a senior', and obeying without grumbling, without contradiction and without any delay. There is no limit to this obedience. The monk obeys up to the point of death, no less. For, writes Columbanus, Christ obeyed the Father right up to death and, however hard may be the orders given to the disciple, he must obey with zeal and gladness even to death, for only so does he take up his cross and follow Christ.

Later in this Rule, in chapter 9, Columbanus deals with the question: suppose the monk believes that the senior's command is mistaken or even morally imperfect? The monk must still obey, as then the responsibility will rest on the senior, and not on the obedient monk. A determination to obey in this way will give the monk peace; humility will protect him. Complete dependence on another, and mortification of his own will and judgement, is the role of the monk.

The modern reader is likely to be struck by two thoughts. First, in the gospels Jesus obeyed God the Father; he did not by any means obey other men; so the monk is making a big leap in his trust and confidence when he takes the order of another man to be that of God to him. Secondly, where does this leave individual conscience, individual responsibility? Could even a medieval monk claim that he was exonerated in doing something he knew was evil simply because he was ordered to do so? Presumably Columbanus would have said 'Yes'.

Three of the provisions in the *Monks' Rule* deal with conditions of their everyday life. Silence is to be maintained as much as possible. It is the seedbed of goodness and peace. Unnecessary talk will lead to such sins as disparaging others and grumbling, all of which break the unity of the community. Very few possessions should content a monk: he should possess on earth only the very few things he absolutely needs, for Columbanus saw a disregard of earthly possessions as a step towards the conquest of faults and vices first, and then on to the love of God. Food and drink should be just sufficient to maintain life. He suggests that one meal of bread and vegetables, in the evening, is adequate. The principle must be of practical usefulness, neither too much nor too little.

After control of the tongue and the appetite the Rule deals with control of the mind. Monks must avoid 'vanity', that is, satisfaction with themselves and with their own work. 'Vanity and proud self-esteem are the destroyer of all good things.' Also the monk guards his mind in chastity. It is not sufficient that his actions are restrained: there must be no sin in his thoughts. Discretion will help us, said Columbanus; discretion is a sober moderation, lighting up God's path for us, illuminating the goodness of the Creator's will, guarding us from stepping aside into extremes, protecting us in temptation.

What purpose could have been served by this short introduction to some of the fundamentals of the religious life? Possibly it was written for beginners, to make sure that they were aware of the difference between life 'in the world' and in the monastery. Seasoned monks would hardly have needed to be reminded of such basics as poverty, chastity, humility, nor of the seedbed of obedience, silence and austerity in which these virtues could grow. But laymen (and many of the Franks wishing to join the monastery would no doubt have been mature men) would have been accustomed to speaking as and when they wished, to a more elaborate and satisfying diet, to finding ways to respond to the normal human desire for riches, to some hope for sexual fulfil-ment, and to acting on their own initiative within the limitations of their daily lives. They would not have been accustomed to a life in which the most important activity was the praise of God in the recitation of the psalms. They would have needed instruction in these things right at the outset of their life in the monastery. If this rule were intended for beginners this would explain why there is no mention of the virtues required by the Abbot or the senior monks.

Chapter 7 gives some details of the choir office, the praise of God which was the most important work of the monk. At first Columbanus is not innovating, but rather basing his provisions on the best practice he has known or read about.

During the working day he makes provision for three short services, at Terce (9.00 a.m.), Sext (midday) and None (3.00 p.m.) Here he is following Cassian closely, and these three offices are deliberately kept short for the same reason as in Cassian: that the work of the day should not be unduly interrupted. So only three psalms are used, to be followed by brief intercessions under six headings: for our sins, for all Christians, for priests and other 'con-secrated' people, for almsgivers, for kings, for our enemies. It seems that Columbanus did not make any use of readings or other prayers in these services.

The main work of prayer was concentrated in the night-hours, which began with a service at dusk and another at midnight, at each of which 12 psalms were used, then gathered its strength for the pre-dawn service, the most important in the 24 hours. Columbanus uses Cassian in determining the number 12 for the psalms in the early part of the night, for Cassian had included a story in which that number had been revealed by an angel. But he abandons Cassian for the pre-dawn service in favour of a system which could have been thought up only by a monk from northern Europe since it makes full use of the great variety, between summer and winter, in the length of the night. Columbanus further makes a difference between the 'holy nights' which lead into Saturday and Sunday and the ordinary nights of the rest of the week. On these ordinary nights at the pre-dawn service 24 psalms would be used in the six months of summer and 36 in the six months of winter. But the 'holy nights' in the height of winter when the nights became longer, this number was gradually increased until, in the depths of winter, 75 psalms were chanted. So, on these two nights of the week in winter, at the pre-dawn service, the whole psalter of 150 psalms was recited. There was nothing like this in Cassian or among the Egyptian monks from whom Cassian took most of his inspiration.

Let the reader then imagine up to 3 hours of continuous psalm-singing before dawn in winter in an unheated chapel, to get some idea of the strength of commitment of Columbanus and his monks to this part of their work. There could not have been any lengthy pause before the whole day began again, and there was no breakfast!

Expert opinion is confident that most of the *Monks' Rule* (with the exception of chapter 10) is a genuine work of Columbanus. Some manuscripts circulated without chapter 7, but that omission could have been because that chapter with its details about the daily services, was felt by the copyists to be not appropriate among general rules, or even because those details had been superseded by later arrangements.

In the absence of any known Rule from an earlier monastery, such as Iona, Columbanus' *Monks' Rule* is taken to be the earliest expression of the monastic ideal to come from an Irish pen. One possible exception is interesting. Around the year 600 a document was produced in Ireland, now called *The Alphabet of Devotion*. This was written in Irish at a time when the Irish language, in addition to Latin, was just beginning to be used in written material. It consists of a number of gentle reflections/recommendations for the practice of the Christian and monastic virtues in a society where there was still some paganism. Occasionally the author became practical and clearly monastic when he recommended 'rising at the first summons' or when he discouraged 'laziness at the bell', 'discourtesy towards a superior' and 'resistance to a prior'. It would be an excellent piece of writing to stimulate meditation or self examination but it would not be possible to deduce from it much about the day-to-day running of a monastery.

It is possible that Columbanus could have known this piece of writing before he left Ireland, since it has no exact date. Perhaps even he met the writer, who is generally thought to have been Colman Elo, a kinsman of Columbanus' own Abbot, Comgall of Bangor. Of all Columbanus' writings the piece that is nearest to the *Alphabet* is Letter 6 (still to be discussed) which is affectionate advice to a young monk on how to live the monastic life.

The Communal Rule

The history of the text of Columbanus' *Communal Rule* is more complicated that that of the *Monks' Rule,* and not all of the text, as it now stands, is attributed to Columbanus. A shorter version, known as the *Short Recension,* is probably his, and the examples which follow are taken from this *Short Recension.* The *Long Recension* contains extras added at a later date.

This Rule is a little like a penitential in that it sets out behaviours to be penalised, and the behaviour to be desired is to be deduced from this. The monk was expected to confess his failures once every day. The time for this was fairly vague: 'before eating or going to bed or whenever it is opportune'. The confession should include very minor faults, to prevent the gradual erosion of standards.

The most common penalties are the physical ones of a number of blows on the hand, or extra fasting. The penalty called 'imposition' appears normally to have been the loss of the evening meal, though it could be an imposed period of silence.

Some examples will give the idea:

Penalised with six blows: not replying Amen to grace at table; speaking unnecessarily at table, or unnecessarily loudly; failing to say a blessing over the spoon; failing to ask a senior to bless the lamp when lit; calling anything one's own; coughing at the beginning of a psalm; smiling during the choir office.

Penalised with twelve blows: not asking for a blessing on leaving the house; forgetting prayer before work or after work; not washing hands before receiving Communion; uttering 'an idle word'.

Penalised with fifty blows: coming too slowly to prayer; speaking with something in the mouth; causing a noise during prayers.

Penalised with fifty blows or an imposition of silence: loud unrestrained speech; telling idle tales to another; defending oneself if accused; contradicting another.

Penalised with an 'imposition', presumably of missing a meal: criticising a brother's work; slandering a brother; speaking abuse in anger; visiting other brothers in their cells; going into the kitchen after nones (the afternoon office); going outside the monastery wall without permission.

Penalised by prostrating oneself in church: spilling some food or drink.

Penalised by fasting for two days on one loaf and water: grumbling; maintaining an argument leading to anger; working carelessly; cutting short the time of one's work.

Penalised by fasting for three days on one loaf: flat refusal of obedience.

Penalised by the recitation of extra psalms as penance: 12 psalms: slandering a lay person, leaving something small outside; not hearing the call to prayer; not shutting the church; 24 psalms: slandering a brother; 30 psalms: leaving something big outside.

Penalised by temporary exclusion from the community: proudly maintaining an argument and involving others. (The brother had to remain in his cell 'until his goodwill is known').

The whole regime may strike a modern reader as ferocious. But when, after Columbanus' death, complaints were made against some of the details of his Rule, these complaints did not include any suggestion that it was too oppressive physically. Presumably any of these prescriptions could be waived at the will of a senior, so the whole system may have been more human than it appears. We may conjecture that medieval people were much more used to the idea of physical violence, in the family, in school and in the judicial system. All the same, there is no doubt that Columbanus' monasteries offered a very strict form of training.

The section of the Penitential dealing with monks adds a number of similarly minor matters, such as leaving the enclosure open, modesty in washing, confession before receiving Communion. It has been observed that it does not seem that Columbanus expected his monks to be involved in any really serious sins (as we might think them). But from such a collection of rules it is possible to see clearly the virtues which he wished to inculcate: obedience, humility, diligence, everything that could help a group of people to live together peacefully, and everything to help the individual monk grow in the Christian life.

Columbanus' Rules leave the readers with questions. For example, we know that he appreciated both beauty and learning and was himself, in the Irish tradition, a very highly educated man. But he does not seem to make space, in the life of his monks, for study. Surely a monk who had gained so much from his own biblical study, and probably had been a teacher if not the principal teacher at Bangor, and, as his letters show, still continued to crave books and presumably to read them, would have wanted others to do the same? But perhaps his Rules never intended to give a complete outline of his monastic plan; perhaps the much more complete and orderly *Rule of St Benedict* has, unfairly, been used as a pattern against which other early Rules are judged. Columbanus wrote within a tradition that was still developing. He did not invent monasticism, and he was well acquainted with the writings of Cassian and some of the works of Basil. It is debated whether he knew and even used the Benedictine Rule. But his writings had to embody and make permanent his own particular emphases. As far as the daily life of the monastery was concerned the living presence of the founding Abbot, and his varying ways of dealing with situations as they arose and giving rulings as they were required, together with his personal charisma and example, would be decisive. The authority of the Abbot was supreme. Columbanus, unlike Benedict, wrote no rules for the conduct of Abbots.

Whether Columbanus' Rules can throw light on the practices of Bangor, from where there is no surviving written Rule, is debateable. The one thing known for certain about Comgall's Bangor was its severity. Columbanus had a strong admiration for the practices of the heroic monks of Ireland. In Letter V he compares them very favourably with the sleepy, spineless Christian warriors of continental Europe! But of course in the day-to-day practices of his own monasteries he would have had to come to terms with continental recruits and their different background. What they thought about it all is shown by the fact that they continued to join him in great numbers.

Monastic life: The Evidence from Jonas
The individual stories in Jonas' hagiography give some picture of life in Columbanus' monasteries: it must be remembered that Jonas was not there, and that this is his impression some thirty years later. Four features stand out:

First, the monks did their own farm-work. There are several farming stories, set at different points in the agricultural year. On one occasion Columbanus went to Fontaines and found sixty 'brethren' hoeing the ground to prepare it for future crop. (These brethren might have included some who were staying there for their time of penance, rather than being regular members of the community.) He found they had very little food and drink, that is, bread and wine, but at his prayer it was multiplied. On another occasion, also at Fontaines, a violent storm was preventing the cutting of a rich crop, but Columbanus stationed men on the perimeter of the field, and himself helped with the harvest in the centre, where they had warm sunshine. At Luxeuil a large number of monks were too ill to work, but when Columbanus nonetheless ordered them to get up and do the threshing those who staggered to their feet to obey were cured. Another time when the harvest was being cut a monk injured his finger so badly that it was almost severed, but when Columbanus had cured his finger he rejoined the work with extra vigour. Cutting and gathering wood was also part of the physical work of the monastery; Columbanus was there in the forest working with the others when a visiting priest was struck on the head by a flying wedge and the saint was able to heal him. The little story of the raven which stole one of Columbanus' gloves gives further evidence, for he wore those gloves when working, and this must mean manual work. A bear had to be warned not to mangle the body of a stag, for the monks needed the hide for shoes, and presumably they were going to make those themselves. The feel of these small details is of a community which sought to be self-sufficient in normal circumstances.

Secondly, there is a little evidence of some organisation within the community. There was a cellarer: the monks made barley-beer and had a cellar to keep it. There was a storehouse for grain; it had a custodian who kept keys and locked the door at night. They ate fish at least on the occasions when they could do their own fishing, but there is no indication as to how they processed it.

Thirdly, the monastery could receive visitors. Obviously the monks must have received kindly those who came for 'the medicine of penance' and those who came to test their vocations. Other visitors mentioned by Jonas included Duke Waldalenus and his wife Flavia, who came to consult about their childlessness, and later to bring their first baby to be baptised by Columbanus. King Theuderic visited, at first in friendly fashion, for he was glad to have the holy man resident in his kingdom, and similarly Columbanus in friendly fashion visited the royal court. But when relations began to sour, after Columbanus' visit to Brunhild's court where he refused to bless the royal bastards, Theuderic began to demand privileges which Columbanus could not grant, such as free access to the whole of the monastery; this shows that the Irish custom was for the monks to have a private enclosure.

Fourthly, Jonas gives us a picture of Columbanus alone. He needed a cell for retreat, fasting and meditation, and found a convenient cave from which the resident bear kindly departed. He was able to bring a fountain of water from the rock in order to meet his need in that cave. Jonas also gives us a picture of Columbanus walking in the woods alone, carrying a book of the Bible and meditating. He managed to escape both wolves and robbers. He made friends with the smaller creatures of the woods, and the impression is that he walked there often.

So, in the small incidentals of his stories (and these are often the most valuable material for historians) Jonas fills out a little, and humanises a little, the severe impression we have from the Rules. We must suppose that these Rules allowed some flexibility in the way they were actually applied. The living Abbot, not the written Rule, was still the ultimate authority. Before we conclude that Columbanus was an ogre we must remember the great personal devotion he inspired, during his life and for a long while after his death.

CHAPTER SEVEN

Relations with the Gallic Bishops

When Columbanus first settled among the Franks he had the permission and support of the local king. There is no suggestion in Jonas' account that he sought also the permission of the local bishop to settle in his diocese. Probably it never occurred to him to do so. In view of the conflict with the Gallic bishops which developed over the next few years and is revealed in Columbanus' letters, though not mentioned by Jonas, we may ask what concept of bishops and their role Columbanus would have brought with him from Ireland.

That bishops were essential for the church was never doubted in Ireland. They, and they alone, could ordain priests and consecrate future bishops. Layfolk received episcopal confirmation after baptism. A document called 'The First Synod of St Patrick', which probably dates from the early sixth century, is clear that the altar of a new church must be consecrated by a bishop before it is used for the Eucharist, and no newcomer to an area may build such a new church without the bishop's permission. A newcomer who is a priest may not baptise or celebrate Mass without permission. But a bishop has authority only in his own *parruchia*; he may not, without his colleague's consent, enter another diocese to ordain or celebrate Mass. There are hints in this document that a bishop has administrative duties also: he has the right to decide the distribution of money given in alms. This writing mentions several occasions when 'permission' is required and when excommunication is imposed or lifted: perhaps this also points to the role of the bishop.

There is no indication in Columbanus' writing that he did not accept any of these rights and duties of bishops in Ireland. One small piece of evidence, in Letter IV, that Columbanus possessed 'the altar that was blessed by the holy bishop Aed' indicated that he accepted this right of a bishop, though we do not know whether Aed, who certainly had an Irish name, travelled with Columbanus, or was otherwise a 'wandering' Irish bishop, or indeed back in Ireland had consecrated a portable altar-stone which Columbanus then brought with him.

But perspectives had been altered in Ireland by the great growth of monasticism, following hard on the heels of the coming of Christianity itself, and by the strength of personality of some of the early Abbots. They were usually not bishops, but many (e.g. the great Columba of Iona) were of commanding moral and intellectual stature and were also aristocrats with powerful family support. They could not be ignored as church leaders. Nor indeed could the kings be ignored in church matters; they were often of the same family as the bishops and abbots, and even in pre-Christian days they were reckoned to be responsible, by maintaining justice, for some of the moral welfare of their people. Also from pre-Christian days an Irish king would have lawyers, and poets who were the guardians of the kingdom's traditions. It would not have seemed possible for any of these to operate alone. In Christian Ireland the great abbots had the same value in society ('honour-price') as kings and bishops; it would have been normal for meetings to include them.

So the word 'synod' to Columbanus would have carried suggestions of the involvement of a wider range of people than such meetings had in the Gallic church. Although the information about Ireland in the days before Columbanus is meagre there are hints in the story of Columba of Iona that he was at one time excommunicated, that this was done at a synod, and also the sentence lifted at a synod, which had at least bishops and abbots present. This synod, which was held at Tailtiu at the same time as the annual 'feast', may have attracted lay attention also. The later synod of Birr (AD 697), where Adomnán promoted his 'law of non-combatants' certainly included bishops, abbots and kings. Although this was a century after Columbanus' departure, it may be an indication of the kind of participation Irishmen expected.

But things were different in Gaul. When Columbanus wrote his second letter, refusing to attend a synod of bishops, perhaps he

would have attended if he had been invited as an equal partici-
pant. Instead it seems that he was summoned as a defendant, and
he would not go.

In Ireland Columbanus could never have met anyone like the
Gallic bishops, in background, family and education. Many were
aristocrats, and some from very distinguished families of Gallo-
Romans of 'senatorial' rank. These were the elite among the
aristocrats. Back in the days of the Roman Empire they had supplied the senators and, as a consequence of that, they provided the
various administrators and governors of the different provinces
and sectors of the Empire. These were families with long traditions of public service: rich, well-educated in the Roman fashion,
civilised, cultured and used to taking a prominent position in
public affairs.

But as the 'barbarians' gradually took over the land there were
fewer opportunities for public service. So these families, now
Christian, sought to fulfil their family traditions of service
through the church by becoming bishops. Every town had its
bishop, and usually, once appointed, he would expect to stay in
the same place for life. So he was able to build up considerable
local knowledge and in fact to become the acknowledged leader
of his town.

On the whole, the Romano-Gallic bishops had an excellent
record of not deserting their towns as the barbarian armies approached, but of staying to negotiate for their people, and often
achieving a workable relationship with the new Frankish lords.
They became the major link between the two societies, Frankish
and Gallo-Roman. A great deal of the administrative and charitable
work of the town was in the hands of the bishop, who therefore
needed managerial skills; fortunately many of them in youth had
had the training appropriate to the landowning and law-giving
class. So bishops did the obvious Christian things, such as caring
for the poor, organising famine relief and the ransom of prisoners,
acting as peacemakers in feuds, building parish churches, and of
course ordaining and training clergy. At this time bishops were
expected to be the main celebrants at the Eucharist and the main
teachers of the faith. But bishops might find themselves also over-

seeing such things as the town walls, the road communications, and aqueducts for the town's water supply. As defenders of Christian moral standards they might have to rebuke the kings, but on the whole they defended kings and tried to work with them, for the kings they had were Catholics, and better a bad Catholic than a good Arian!

Columbanus of course had absolutely no experience in Ireland of this kind of bishop, and Jonas seems to have had a poor opinion of them. Jonas asserts that when Columbanus arrived in Gaul 'either because of the numerous enemies from without, or on account of the carelessness of the bishops, the Christian faith had almost departed from the country' (I 11). Christianity was dead in Gaul until his hero revived it! But this view must be questioned in order to get a more balanced picture of what Columbanus actually achieved.

The life of Gregory of Tours gives an example of a bishop who certainly was not careless. He was almost contemporary with Columbanus, dying in 594, three years after Columbanus arrived in Gaul. Gregory was from a very distinguished family of Gallo-Romans which had supplied a great number of bishops to the Frankish church. He tells us that thirteen of the eighteen bishops of Tours who preceded him were his blood-relatives, not counting a large number of bishops of other towns! He was almost born into the job. As a bishop he seems to have been brave, caring and conscientious. Unusually, but very usefully for us, he had the urge to write, and he wrote not in the complicated style of many of his class but in a straightforward, 'rustic' style of Latin. His most famous book, now called *The History of the Franks,* gives a graphic picture of his own times, dramatic and bloodthirsty. It is not the work of a man who was indifferent to the evils around him.

But Gregory of Tours was not a monk and does not write much about monasteries. It is in the monasteries that the saints of Gaul can be found, and these monasteries are worth a detailed description in order to modify Jonas' bad impression and to enable Columbanus' achievement to be assessed and appreciated.

Over the monastic movement in Gaul brooded the spirit of St Martin of Tours, still very powerful in the sixth century although he had died in c.400. He was the first to attempt to combine the life of a monk with the office of a bishop, and later monk-bishops played an important role in Gaul and elsewhere. Martin was born in the eastern half of the Empire in about 315; his father, an officer in the Roman army, was a keen pagan. But about the age of ten the child found himself attracted to a meeting of the Christians – so attracted that by his middle teens he wanted nothing more than to live as a hermit in the desert. His father, though, had other ideas and arranged for him to be recruited into the Roman army. Martin seems to have completed the usual length of army service, until his early 40s, then, for a while, he became a hermit, eventually settling near Poitiers with the friendly support of the bishop, attracting companions and becoming well-known for gifts of spiritual healing. So, when a vacancy for a bishop occurred in near-by Tours he was appointed by popular acclaim (after an uneasy moment when other bishops of the area expressed their upper-class disapproval of someone so unkempt, so uneducated and of such dubious background). As Bishop of Tours Martin did not live in the bishop's house in the city, but retired to a nearby field, lived there as a monk in a hut, and walked in to Tours daily to fulfil his duties as bishop. Inevitably he attracted disciples and an early type of monastic community grew up. As bishop, Martin had a substantial healing ministry; he also had a developed sense of pastoral care for his clergy and spent his winters walking (!) round his diocese, visiting the clergy and assisting them in any difficulties. On one such expedition he died, an aged man; his body was taken to Tours and became the centre of a substantial cult, with churches dedicated to him throughout much of western Europe including Britain.

After Martin's death the number of monk-bishops multiplied in Gaul, and the reason was a monastery which specialised in producing them. This was Lérins, a tiny island in the Mediterranean quite close to Marseilles. Here, in about 420, an aristocrat named Honoratus, with a number of his relatives and friends, all aristocrats, had founded an ascetic community. These monks did not do manual work, though they did distribute alms to the poor. They lived a life of obedience and humility under a superior. But

Lérins soon became a very important cultural centre. Most of its members would have had the secular education given to boys of their class, emphasising skill in a Latin which was not only correct but also beautiful and persuasive. To this they added study of the Bible and of the early Christian Latin writings, and in time the monastery evolved its own spiritual tradition. But its most important contribution was in the number of its members who, having the basic training of a monk, then became bishops. As such they were fulfilling the aristocratic ideal of public service and also made known and made popular the monastic and ascetic ideals. Many Gallic towns competed to acquire a bishop trained at Lérins.

It is possible to make quite of long list of Lérinian bishops of Gaul during the fifth century, but one of the most influential belongs rather to the first half of the sixth, nearer to the arrival of Columbanus. This was Caesarius of Arles. Born into an aristocratic family he chose to break away in his late teens and joined Lérins at the age of 19. But after practising an over-enthusiastic asceticism his health gave way, and the Abbot arranged for him to go to Arles, where the bishop was a relative. Caesarius did not return to Lérins, but when he became bishop himself of this very important town of Arles, which had been a centre of Roman administration, he still continued to live with great simplicity. In time he was made Metropolitan, the equivalent of an Archbishop, presiding over synods, advising other bishops, endeavouring to settle disputes among Christians and negotiating with the barbarian rulers. He founded two monasteries in Arles, for monks and nuns respectively. The Abbess of the nuns was his sister Caesaria and he wrote a Rule for that community. But a major interest of his was in preaching, in which, unlike some highly-educated aristocrats, he cultivated a very simple style. His sermons were widely copied and used by others, a practice of which he approved, and he is said to have spent useful mealtimes with his clergy catechising them about what they had learnt and remembered. But the time he died in 542 Lérins was in decline, but Caesarius is an example of living vigorous Christianity only fifty years before Columbanus arrived, and he was not the last.

Bishops who were trained in monasteries but then had close

involvement in the day-to-day life of the church prevented a possibly dangerous split with the bishops and their flocks on the one
side and the monastic movement on the other. But this was a time
of experiments in monasticism, and some monastic founders in
Gaul had different ideals, with no intention of involvement in the
daily life of the church. The monastery of Agaune, far from civilisation at the foot of the pass over the Alps known as the Great St
Bernard, was founded by a Burgundian prince, Sigismund, who
died in 524. He took the advice of various bishops in choosing the
spot and the monastic life was influenced in part by Byzantine
models. The most distinctive feature of this monastery was the
laus perennis, 'perpetual praise': the monks were divided into
groups and took it in turn to sing the praise of God in their liturgy,
so that there was no moment of the day or night when some members of the monastery were not so engaged. So Agaune was a specialist house; the monks were not drawn from the locality but
from elsewhere; they often had previous monastic experience but
then chose to concentrate on the Agaune way of serving God. The
monastery would have been richly endowed with privileges and
lands.

But one set of three monasteries in the Jura mountains represented yet a different way of being monks. These communities
were founded by Romanus in 435 to live in the real desert far from
any normal route or contact with civilisation. Romanus himself
was of good family, and was subsequently joined by both his
brother and his sister, as one of the three monasteries was for
women. But the way of life was hostile to the civilised aristocracy
of Gaul. It involved contemplation and reading, but also hard
physical work; it involved both rich and poor, a common life
(dormitories etc.) and a very basic standard of living. Of course it
attracted pilgrims, especially those who admired what they saw
as primitive ideals and even some resemblance to the toughness
of the old Roman spirit, and it built up a reputation for healings
and exorcisms. But impressive as it was it did not lead to many
imitations.

Meanwhile, what about the women? We have mentioned religious houses for women founded by men. But much nearer to the

time of Columbanus' arrival in Gaul was the life of the principal woman saint of the sixth century, Radegund, who died in 587, just four years before the coming of the Irish group. She was a Thuringian princess who, having been captured in war, had come into the possession of Chlothar, King of the Franks. He gave her a good education, in literacy among other things, with a view to making her his queen. But even as a child she had other ideas and played at being a nun. As a teenager she was forcibly married to Chlothar, but lived an ascetic life as much as she possibly could, slipping away from the royal bedroom for prayer during the night, giving generously in alms, and even caring for the poor and diseased with her own hands. But after Chlothar murdered her brother who had been her fellow-captive she fled from the court and the king was eventually persuaded to relinquish his claim on her and even to support her in her desire to found a community at Poitiers, which he did generously.

The poet Venantius Fortunatus wrote a *Vita* of Radegund which was supplemented by an account written by one of her nuns, Baudovinia. Gregory of Tours knew her well and included some information in his *Decem Libri*. These writings give a picture of her intensely ascetic life: torturing practices inflicted on her own body, extreme fasting, physical care for the poor. Although a king's daughter and formerly a queen she did not rule in her own monastery but obeyed another, Sister Agnes, as Abbess, and took her share in all the often dirty work of cleaning, cooking etc. But of course neither she nor others could forget who she was and what was her previous experience. She introduced intercessory prayer into the nuns' regime, especially for kings in their constant war-fare, of which she would have been more aware than the majority of cloistered women. She introduced also the Rule which Caesarius of Arles had drawn up for his sister Caesaria. Most dramatically she desired a relic of the True Cross (said to have been discovered by Helena, mother of the Emperor Constantine) and with the king's permission requested and obtained a frag-ment of it from the Emperor in Constantinople. The relic was brought into the monastery with great pageantry which gave the poet Fortunatus the opportunity to write two famous hymns:

'Sing, my tongue, the glorious battle' and 'The royal banners forward go'. It is possible that the acquisition of this relic was one of the causes of the coldness towards the Monastery of the Holy Cross, as it was now called, by the Bishop of Poitiers, Meroveus, who may well have felt undermined by Radegund's fame, which was increased by the large number of miracles attributed to her, and eventually by other poems of Fortunatus, who lived within the shadow of her community and in time became Bishop of Poitiers himself. He seems to have had an affectionate but entirely proper relationship with Radegund and the picture of her austerity is modified a little by the conversations they enjoyed and the gifts they exchanged.

It seems difficult to believe that a Gaul which contained these interesting religious movements and colourful characters was quite as dead as Jonas implies. We must allow him the freedom of a hagiographer to shape his material in order to present his 'hero' as he wishes. However, the Gallo-Roman religious houses described, with other early monasteries, had been mostly in the south, mostly situated in cities and towns, strongly aristocratic and under the protection and guidance of the bishops. Columbanus and his disciples, Franks rather than Gauls, founded monasteries further north, in the country, and open to everyone. So he was contributing something new and different.

In the letter in which he declined to attend the bishops' synod (Letter 2) Columbanus does not deal specifically with any problems they might have about him. He rather asks simply that he and his monks should be left alone, to live as pilgrims in the traditions of their (Irish) ancestors. There will be room, he says, for all of us in heaven, so why not in Gaul?

But the bishops did have problems with him, of which the greatest was his determination to stick to his ancestral tradition on the question of calculating the date of Easter. He maintained his intransigence on this to the end of his life.

Modern people tend to think that the problem of the date of Easter is a trivial one and could have been easily settled because the calendar is a human invention and could be altered to suit human convenience. No Christian of earlier centuries would have thought so. They believed that, just as God had chosen all the interventions in the story of his Chosen People which are recorded in the Old Testament, so he had chosen both the place and the time for the incarnation of his Son and especially for the great act of redemption, Jesus' death and resurrection. Further, God had left sufficient evidence of his will for the celebration of these supreme events, the most important events in the whole of human history. The proper response for human beings was to discover God's will and obey it. Those Christians, such as the Irish but many others also, who put obedience to God as the foundation of their spirituality would be the most concerned to find the right way.

As everyone agreed that Jesus died and rose again at Passover time they scrutinised the regulations for the Passover. This was a very ancient feast going back to those shadowy beginnings of the Hebrew people when they were nomads with flocks and herds. In early spring they set out to move to their summer pastures but the newborn animals were delicate so the operation was an anxious one; they moved by night and needed the brilliant light of the first spring full-moon. Before they moved they performed a ceremony to ensure their safety. But one year, when the people had gone down to Egypt and then been enslaved there, the Passover took on a new dramatic meaning. They believed that God had inflicted a plague, the death of the first-born, on the Egyptians to release the Hebrews and lead them, under Moses, to freedom in a different land. Passover then became the celebration of freedom and, centuries later when they were oppressed by the Romans, Passover became the focus for the hope of a new act of liberation.

The date of Passover was not a problem. Just by watching the sky in the first month of spring they could count 14 nights from the night when the new moon became visible. That was Passover, a single feast on the night of the full moon, and in a little country like Palestine it was easy for everyone to be informed of the date in advance.

But when the Hebrews settled in the land of Canaan and began to be arable farmers they celebrated another spring festival, that of Unleavened Bread. This lasted seven days and symbolised the clearing out of the old crops and preparation for the new. It was added to the Feast of the Passover, but one Old Testament source,

Deuteronomy, began the seven days on the day of the Passover and another, Leviticus, began the following day. The dates of the combined festival then were either 14th-20th of the first spring (lunar) month or 14th-21st.

The New Testament did not really add any complications. Although the first three gospels think of the Last Supper as the Passover meal, whereas John thinks it was the day before, this was not a major problem. All agreed that Jesus had kept the Last Supper on a Thursday evening, had died on a Friday and risen on a Sunday, all at Passover time.

The problems began when the early church decided that Easter should always be on a Sunday, so detaching it from the feast of the Passover, which could be on any night of the week. Only a very small group of Christians insisted on keeping to the 14th day. The other found a formula on which all could agree: that Easter is the first Sunday after the first full moon after the spring equinox. This formula is still in use.

Some problems then arose through different understanding of some of the terms in this formula. When is the spring equinox? The continental Christians eventually settled for March 21st, and, scientifically, were right. But the Irish believed the equinox was March 25th. Of course if first the full moon and then a Sunday happened between 21st and 25th to the continentals that Sunday would be Easter; the Irish would wait another month because the equinox had not yet occurred. Why did it matter? Because before the equinox the night was marginally longer than the day, and the vital all-important symbolism of Easter was the victory of light over darkness, of good over evil, of life over death.

Because Easter was always on a Sunday it would happen sometimes that the feast of the Passover would happen on the same Sunday. So could the Christians keep that Sunday as Easter? The Irish Christians said 'yes'. Columbanus himself remarks that since the Jews do not keep Easter what does it matter to the Christians what they do? But the continental Christians said 'no' and preferred to wait another week. There were no Jews in Ireland but many places on the continent had large Jewish populations, and there the Christians were anxious that the pagans would be able to see clear difference between Christians and Jews. But, the Irish objected, this would move Easter outside the Deuteronomy dates of Nisan 14th-20th, which they followed. After Nisan 21st the moon would be visible for less than half of the night. This again would disturb the symbolism of Easter, the victory of light over darkness. Columbanus protests that Christians cannot possibly celebrate 'a dark Easter'.

But Christians, unlike Jews, needed to know the date of Easter in advance, so that they could begin Lent. So the mathematicians of the early church began the complex task of producing mathematical tables, to bring together the timetable of the sun (to give the equinox) and the timetable of the moon. Several such tables were in time produced, but did not always agree. One of the difficulties between the Irish and the continentals was that the Irish were still using tables which the continentals considered had been superseded by better ones.

But if Christians could not agree on all of this, did it matter? It seems from Columbanus' letters, which are our earliest evidence for the Irish position, that he moved from his first position of requiring the rest of the world to agree that the Irish were right to a second position of asking only that the Irish should not be persecuted for taking a different line. To the end of his life he clung to 'the tradition of the (Irish) elders'. But the continental Christians were looking for unity. They wanted the church to show a united front to new converts, and indeed to show solidarity in doctrine and in custom. They lived in a wider world, facing challenges the Irish did not have to meet.

It is possible that continental Christians did not know about difficulties in Ireland over these questions until Columbanus arrived with his different ideas. So it seems very reasonable that they should invite him to a synod to explain himself, especially about the date of Easter. He did not go, and if he had not been supported by the kings it is more that likely that the bishops would have succeeded in expelling him from their territory.

Later, after his death, the inevitable happened and the Columbanian monasteries accepted the continental dating of Easter.

CHAPTER EIGHT

In Francia: The Credentials of Sainthood

In writing a hagiography, Jonas set out to give the evidence for claiming that his subject was indeed a saint. This could be of two kinds: first, the simple goodness of those who were living the gospel life and, secondly, the special powers from God with which the saint was endowed.

Jonas does not undervalue the first. His picture of the little community when they arrived in Gaul shows his ideals: humility, common ownership, common concern for each other, sharing of the hard work, no harsh words. To people outside it was attractive, 'People must have believed that an angelic life was being lived by mortal men.' Columbanus' own presence was sufficient to make those who met him resolve to be better Christians.

But the spiritual powers, the ability both to work and to receive 'miracles', were very important, and Jonas supplies stories of them on nearly every page. Several times the monks were almost at starvation. God might inspire a wealthy person to send help. So, to give one example among many, when an unnamed man arrived at the gate with horses loaded with food he was rewarded by prayer which healed his sick wife. Sometimes the monks' needs were met without a human agent: in response to prayer water came from a rock, or an empty and locked storehouse was found next morning to be full of grain. The need might not be of food: when soldiers came to remove Columbanus on royal orders he was strangely invisible and could not be taken until he agreed to go. All this would maintain the picture of a community living under God's protection.

The gift of healing was another major spiritual power, and Jonas gives several examples. Some of these healings were done through close contact: a monk almost lost a finger while reaping, but Columbanus restored it and the monk later showed the finger to Jonas. A parish priest watching the monks foresting was hit on the head by a flying timber wedge, but Columbanus healed the wound with his saliva. Some healings were done at a distance, and sometimes whole groups came to Columbanus and were healed.

Many stories of the saint's spiritual gifts are 'nature-miracles', involving either animals or the inanimate forces of nature. The animals encountered by Columbanus are of two kinds: the little harmless ones with which he could have friendship and the large dangerous ones over which he must exercise control. In the first group Jonas paints a charming picture of Columbanus walking in the woods and calling the small birds and beasts; they would frisk around him and allow him to stroke them. In particular he could whistle down a squirrel from the top of the trees, and the little animal would sit on his hand, curl around his neck, and burrow under his cloak. But he could be severe even with animals. Among the birds the raven still had a bad reputation, since it did not return to Noah when he sent it on reconnaissance from the Ark. So when Columbanus lost a glove he knew exactly who would have taken it and declared that the thief would not be able to feed its young. Sure enough the penitent raven returned the glove!

Among the larger animals the dangerous ones were wolves and bears, still roaming in the Vosges mountains at this time. Columbanus had an early encounter with twelve wolves which surrounded him and seized his clothes. But since he showed no fear, but stood absolutely still and prayed while they came right up and investigated him, they lost interest and wandered away. Three episodes with bears are narrated: first, a bear occupied a cave which Columbanus wanted as a place of retreat, but left without argument at his command; secondly, a bear was about to devour the body of a stag but withdrew because Columbanus and his monks needed the hide; thirdly, a bear in an orchard of wild apples was content at the word of the saint to be confined for its food to one section of the orchard and leave the rest for the monks.

Other nature-miracles concern inanimate forces. One time a monk was in the act of pouring beer from a jar when the saint called for him. Anxious to show perfect obedience, the supreme virtue of a monk, he went, forgetting to put the plug back into the jar. But the beer stopped flowing of its own accord and nothing was lost. Such is the power of obedience or, as they would have said, the power of God in response to this virtue. The element of water was usually on Columbanus' side. As previously mentioned, it regulated itself to prevent the saint's deportation to Ireland.

Some of the stories about Columbanus' special powers could be called 'miracles of judgement'. After the argument about the blessing of the king's sons, as Columbanus left, there was a loud cracking noise which to Jonas was meant to instil fear. Later in the story, just outside the city of Bregenz, Columbanus encountered pagans with huge cask of beer for a heathen offering. He breathed on it, the cask broken open with a crash spilling all the beer, and some of the people there became Christians.

A further spiritual gift which appears particularly in the latter part of the story is the gift of prophecy. Columbanus had indeed used this earlier to foretell the birth of children to a childless duke and his wife who asked him to pray for them. Also, in visiting other noble families, he pronounced a prophetic blessing on some of their children. But towards the end of his time in Francia the prophecy is of destruction and death. During his forced voyage as a captive on his way to Nantes, he prophesised the death of a guard who attacked one of his companions gratuitously: the man later died at the place where Columbanus said he would. But most prophecies of destruction were about his royal enemies, specially in support of the friendly Frankish King Chlothar against his enemies Theuderic and Theudebert. The latter indeed had not been the saint's enemy but he did die as predicted.

Converse with angels was also expected of a saint. Jonas has only one angel-story: an angel was sent to assist Columbanus to decide what to do next, when it was becoming clear that he must leave Frankish territory. The angel's words are not specifically directive, but to Columbanus they encouraged the idea of going to Italy.

With this kind of story on almost every page the appetite of the original reader would be satisfied. But he would have been very surprised, at the end of the book, to find no accounts of miracles performed by the saint at his tomb. Such miracles stories were considered essential by hagiographers, as they were presented as evidence that the saint had indeed arrived in heaven and so was a proper object for prayers and a cult. Jonas does mention very briefly that Columbanus' remains did in fact exercise 'powers'. But Jonas has planned to write a second book and so proceeds to this.

CHAPTER NINE

Columbanus at Milan and Bobbio

Columbanus' journey over the Alps, when he had been expelled from their territory by the Frankish royal family, took him to North Italy, the area known as Lombardy. The Lombards were another group of Germanic 'barbarians' who had infiltrated from the north and settled. In religion they were a mixture of pagans and Arian Christians (see ch 4). Their chief city was Milan and it seems that Columbanus went there to meet Agilulf, King of the Lombards, who received him kindly and allowed him to stay. Agilulf's own religious position is vague, but he seems not to have been a militant Arian, and according to Jonas Columbanus was not hindered in preaching against Arianism.

It is likely that Columbanus had not actually met Arianism before, though he may have heard about it. He would, of course, have reacted against it with horror. His own writings, especially Sermon 1, show that the Catholic doctrines of the incarnation and the Trinity were first in his list of essential beliefs. Even if King Agilulf was technically an Arian Columbanus would have had an ally in the Queen, Theodolinda, who was a firm Catholic.

She was, however, a supporter of the 'Three Chapters' schism, which Columbanus encountered in Milan also. The three chapters in question were some of the writings of three Christian thinkers from an earlier century: Theodore of Mopsuestia (died 428), Theodoret of Cyrrhus and Ibas of Edessa. Their works dealt with one of the major problems of the church in the early centuries, which was to arrive at an agreed way of answering the question: how could Jesus be both God and Man? How did the incarnation 'work'? In this debate, some theologians tended to stress the Manhood, others the Godhead, of the incarnate Christ. Modern historians for the sake of convenience have labelled these two tendencies 'Antiochene' and 'Alexandrian'. The Antiochenes stressed the genuine and complete human nature of Christ, including the reality of his moral struggles, and also the importance of the literal and historical interpretation of the scriptures. The Alexandrians stressed the unity of the Godhead and Manhood of Christ. Both were right, but both could easily lose balance.

The writers of the 'three chapters' were all of Antiochene outlook but, during their lives, none had been condemned as a heretic. The schism arose through the initiative of the Emperor Justinian (died 565). As a Roman Emperor at Constantinople, but a Christian, he considered that his authority covered both church and state and that it was his duty to pronounce on matters of Christian doctrine as well as politics. So, in part to please those many of his subjects who were Alexandrian in their thinking, especially in the eastern part of the Empire, he organised the condemnation of the three chapters.

But Christians in the western part of the Empire did not so easily accept the religious authority of the Emperor, who to them may have appeared a remote eastern figurehead. At Rome the Pope of the time, Vigilius, hesitated and even suffered a period of imprisonment by the Emperor before he finally accepted this decision. But his acceptance outraged some of the western bishops who went into schism against the Pope, and this dispute had not been solved by the time Columbanus arrived in Milan. He was appalled at the damage to the church, and this is the occasion of the writing of his fifth letter, addressed to Pope Boniface IV.

How much he understood of the background to the schism is not clear. He does not mention the Emperor. Perhaps the whole idea of and spirit of Easter Christianity was hazy to him. He accepts fully the authority of the Pope, provided that the Pope is not himself a heretic. (Columbanus had heard a malicious whisper to that effect while he was in Milan, but he did not wish to believe it.) He sees the church in very great peril and is ready to condemn the bad leadership which had got it there.

It is a strange letter and has been evaluated differently by historians, some of whom had stressed its impertinence and others its flattery. Probably Columbanus did not intend either. He knows that he is an unknown man, and a newcomer to the Italian scene.

He stresses the total Catholic orthodoxy of his own church back in Ireland, where he had seen wonderful examples of sainthood. He stresses also the gratitude of the Irish to Christian Rome, from where they first received the faith: perhaps here he had the mission of Palladius in mind (ch 2). But back in Ireland what mattered had not been a man's social or ecclesiastical position, but rather his devotion and his principles. So, as a concerned brother Christian, he can recall the Pope to his duty. So he urges him to wake up, to clear himself of the charge of heresy, to use his authority vigorously to save the church which is like a ship in danger of imminent shipwreck. He seems to think that if both sides of the dispute are brought together to consider the matter they will soon see and agree on the truth. He also urges the Pope to write to King Agilulf, who could easily be persuaded, presumably to the full Catholic understanding of the Christian faith.

There is no recorded answer to this letter, or any indication that it had results. Perhaps Columbanus never did understand the situation. But it is worth noting that this earliest Irish Christian voice is so positive about the position of Rome and so grateful. Columbanus knows that he is a fringer, and like many fringers he longs to belong to and be accepted by the centre. There is no trace here of any antagonism between Rome and 'the Celts'.

The foundation of Bobbio

Columbanus did not intend to stay in Milan: he wished to found another monastery and depended on the king to grant some land for this. Jonas tells of an otherwise unknown man, Jocundus, who appeared at the king's court and suggested for Columbanus a place in the Apennines called Bobbio, where there was a disused church dedicated to St Peter. The place was fertile and there were two rivers in the neighbourhood. It is clear that the king already knew the place since the text of the document in which he granted the church and its neighbouring land to Columbanus has survived, and Agilulf has to make an exception of half a salt-pit there, which he had already granted to a certain Sundrarit. So Columbanus went to Bobbio, liked it and founded there his last monastery.

Jonas tells us very little of the saint's life at Bobbio. The church was somewhat ruinous, though it had been a building of beauty which Columbanus restored. The actual building work was accompanied, says Jonas, by a miracle in which the monks, including the Abbot, were given supernatural strength to carry the timber from the cliffs and dense woods. Jonas also recounts that Columbanus at Bobbio received an invitation from Chlothar (the Frankish king who was his friend) to go back 'home' to the Franks, for he had exterminated the whole family of Columbanus' enemy Theuderic, including Brunhild, and was now king of all the Frankish territory. But the now aging saint did not feel that he could make the journey over the Alps again. So he wrote to Chlothar asking him to give his support and protection to the monastery at Luxeuil under Abbot Eustasius, who himself had brought the king's invitation and took back the reply. The King reacted very positively and gave every possible support to Luxeuil.

Apart from this brief information, Jonas mentions only Columbanus' death about a year after he had come to Bobbio. However, there is another source, the *Miracula Sacti Columbani*. This document was written by an anonymous monk of Bobbio in the tenth century and deals mainly with a number of miracles worked by St Columbanus' body, some 300 years after his death, to safeguard the property of the monastery which was under threat. The document has many disadvantages: it was written in rather poor Latin prose, it was added to and mangled by a later hand, it was written so long after the saint's life at Bobbio. But it may have preserved through oral tradition some genuine material from those first days.

It tells that Columbanus chose a spot a little distant from the monastery, to build there an oratory 'to fit his own size!' This tiny church was dedicated to the Blessed Virgin. Outside it he erected a free-standing cross. The author says that the saint spent the whole of Lent there and most weekdays also. Whether this would have really been possible for an active Abbot may be doubted, but perhaps Columbanus, now in his last year, was already 'in retirement'.

The little building itself continued to stand for some centuries, and the story gains support from a number of considerations: we know from Jonas (I 15) that Columbanus, even at the height of his strength and activity, did from time to time retire to a cave or other retreat for prayer. We know also that free-standing crosses, objects of veneration, were part of the Irish tradition, and that tiny churches in stone (more durable than the original wood) still exist in those places where wood for building was not available. In maintaining the tradition of the 'hermit' alongside that of the 'active' monk, Columbanus was continuing faithful to his Irishness to the end.

The Thirteen Sermons

While he was at Milan, or perhaps more probably at Bobbio, Columbanus wrote and preached the thirteen sermons which have been preserved among his other writings. As these sermons move coherently in progression of ideas it is likely that they were composed as a set, and in the order in which they have been preserved. The manuscript evidence supports this, for the major manuscripts used by scholars contain the thirteen sermons in this order. Perhaps the sermons were intended as a kind of 'last testament'. The Irish did not write books of 'spirituality' but these sermons can be read as Columbanus' witness to that in the Christian faith which he believed to be the most important and to which he hoped his community would be faithful.

His teaching may be presented as answers to a number of questions:

1) What do we mean by 'God'?

Nothing less or other than the full doctrines of the Trinity and the incarnation as set out in the Creeds. Columbanus believed these doctrines to be clearly revealed in the scriptures, but he forbade further speculation as to exactly how these things can be understood. Doctrinal disputes over details were occupying and rending the eastern half of the church at this time, but they did not appeal to the Irish mind, and Columbanus had a horror of uncharitable argument.

In his emphasis on the awesomeness and unknowability of

God he is close to what was later called the 'apophatic' tradition, with its strong emphasis on how little we know and
its avoidance of over-confidently positive statements about
God and his nature. He is in the company, for example, of
the 14th century English writer of *The Cloud of Unknowing*,
who remarks laconically of God: 'By love he may be gotten
and holden, but by thought never.' It has often been noted
that the Irish were practical rather than theoretical, not interested in doctrinal or systematic theology. Their tradition
produced only one great Christian philosopher, Eriugena, in
the 9th century.

2) How do we know this about God?

Not by discussion or speculation, but solely by obedience
to his will. The Irish approached biblical studies, on which
they were extremely keen, with the practical question,
'How does God want us to live?' Then they went out to try
to live like that.

For Columbanus 'knowing' God meant living in his way. In
this he is standing firmly within the Hebrew tradition of the
Old Testament.

3) Who or what is our main enemy in seeking to live this life?

Our own weakness and stupidity. It is noteworthy that
Columbanus did not blame the devil or the demons. As a bib-
lically-minded Christian he did of course accept the reality
of both but, in comparison for instance with the stories of
the Desert Fathers, he was remarkably free from demon-
awareness. This is true of the Irish tradition generally.

Columbanus had just one brief reference to his monks as soldiers, fighting a spiritual warfare against spiritual foes. Mostly
their striving was with and against themselves.

4) What do we need to overcome this human weakness?

Columbanus believed two things were needed: first, a
realisation, frequently renewed in the monks' minds, of the
happiness to which they were destined. They were living
now in the company of God, partially to be known here. But
they were moving towards the full knowledge of and full
enjoyment of his presence, with all that that meant for their

own happiness and fulfilment. They were moving towards their own true home, which never could be found here on this earth.

Columbanus did not hesitate to hold out heaven as a reward. He did not at any point say that the physical world is itself evil, but only that it is temporary and worth only temporary love. But the reward was not separate from the choice. Heaven did not come automatically; there was judgement. But, he said, the monks have made the best possible choice, so they can travel happily to an end which was glorious beyond all that they could know. The reward could be experienced in some measure here, and in full measure there. Secondly, his monks must have a sober realisation that to overcome their weakness and self-will they need an apprenticeship, a period of solid training. All apprenticeship could have its dull and difficult moments. He did not minimise the effort involved. Life had to be cleansed of rubble and this could take a lifetime. He emphasised the impermanence of the world and the need to choose decisively. Although all training was difficult Christian training was for the best possible end.

5) How then do we view our lives?

Columbanus' major metaphor was 'life is a road on which we are travellers'. So, he says, the monks must fix their minds on the goal: life was not aimless but going somewhere. But they must live like travellers; they do not carry unnecessary luggage but must be content with a traveller's allowance; they must turn away from distractions and not be diverted by others who choose differently; they must not sit down on the road to rest or pause, much less to set up house there; they must believe in God's mercy but not presume on it; they must reject and fight evil in all its forms. This metaphor of life as a road was to have a long Christian history. The most developed use of it was in Bunyan's *Pilgrim's Progress*, where exactly the same points are made.

So Columbanus' spirituality (which is our earliest evidence for Irish monastic spirituality) is very tough. In a sense it is narrow.

He picks up the biblical idea of the 'two ways' and chooses the narrow way which leads to life. The Jesus who appears in these sermons is the Jesus who followed the Father's will all the way to death and who called on his disciples to do the same. Columbanus does not write about the Jesus who enjoyed going out to dinner-parties and had easy friendships with women. But it would not be right to call Columbanus' outlook 'grim' for he has a clear appreciation of the happiness which awaits them at the end of the journey. But in this life commitment through the monastic way is total. What his last words were is not known, but if he had only two words to gasp out as his last message they might have been 'persist' and 'endure'.

The death of Columbanus

It would have been good to have more about Columbanus' last days. Jonas is astonishingly brief. Of course he was not there himself at the time but plenty of others, still alive when he wrote, had been there. But all that Jonas gives is the date of his death (thought to be 23 November 615), a recommendation to read his writings, and the fact that he was buried at Bobbio. The medieval reader would have expected some account of miracles performed at or near his tomb by the saint in heaven. Jonas does indeed mention there: '(his remains) have proved their virtues, by the aid of Christ', where 'virtues' would mean the power of God flowing through the earthly remains to work the same kind of miracles of healing etc as the saint performed during his life. But no examples are given of these.

Jonas proceeds to write his second book, which has a different theme.

(As an appendix to this chapter a précis of the 13 sermons is provided: each paragraph summarises a sermon. This is for the interest of the reader who would like to follow through Columbanus' thinking. Better still, read the full text in Walker's edition!)

APPENDIX ONE: PRECIS OF THE SERMONS

1) My brothers, we begin with the most important thing of all to us, our faith in God. About God we believe what he himself has revealed to us: that he is one, existing as the Trinity of Father, Son and Holy Spirit, infinite and eternal, utterly vast, yet present to even the smallest creature; he is both immeasurably far off and inconceivably close. Believing this gives us enough to live the life of faith. How arrogant it would be to seek to know God's inner secrets, mysteries of his life, power and way of existence. And how futile! Our small minds are not made for that. Think of this world, our familiar earth and sea: familiar indeed, and how much we know of them, and yet how little. What do we know of the teaming life beneath the waves, or even on much of the surface of the earth? No, we can't grow close to God by speculation or by discussion. But he has given us another way in which we can indeed grow close to him, and that is by choosing to live as he wants us to live. So seek to live in his way! Our journey through this world is bound to be in semi-darkness, until he brings us out into the glorious world of his presence, to which he is leading us.

2) So we ponder all the light we have been given in his word. Beyond this we do not expect to have knowledge, and certainly not from so-called 'teachers' who go beyond God's word. Listen for a moment to a good teacher, named Faustus, who speaks (in a parable) of the work of a competent farmer, who is not content to sow seed in land which has been ploughed unless it has also been cleaned of weeds and rubble. In our life we must root out vices and plant virtues, for our religion is of no use if it stays on the outside: it must penetrate to our hearts, to the very centre of our lives. So we, as far as we can, must free ourselves from pride, anger and other such 'rubble', and we must plant peace, gentleness, joy and love. It's pointless just to read and hear about these things; we have got to live them, and this is very hard work; it is real toil, needing a lot of patience and persistence. It is the work of a lifetime, a constant striving. Indeed it can be called a sort of warfare, and for success in this warfare, if we fight on his side his grace will be with us and help us.

3) We are seeking the very best thing in the world. What is that? Can there be anything better than to please God by living according to his will? We must apply ourselves to this, but we shall be helped by a true understanding of what is real and permanent in life. For when we look at the physical world in which we live nothing is permanent. All living things decline and die, and that includes us. But God has given to us human beings a chance to live differently, by choosing to set our hearts not on the things that die, but on the things that live for ever. Only by living well, by living according to God's will, can we possess eternal values and move towards eternal life. So we must first see clearly the things we must not love, the desires and vices which draw us down to a spiritual death. What could be more wretched than to live the life which is itself a kind of death and which ends inevitably in real death of body and soul? So, make a vigorous choice. Reject decisively the things that lead you away from God, earthly and transitory things, pomp, mirth, lust. You have an eternal treasure, your self, your soul, which is worth your love. Love yourself rightly, love yourself enough to choose your own happiness in choosing the way of God.

4) Of course it won't be easy. It will be very difficult, for it is God's way of training us for eternity, and our own stupid and weak selves get in the way. But think of the people you have known who have undertaken some kind of apprenticeship to learn a trade or skill. Was it always easy for them? Did they always find learning pleasant? No, often they had to force themselves, or be forced by their master, to buckle down to it. But they hoped for the happiness of becoming a master themselves. Indeed, if they got there it was a joyful achievement. Except, of course, that they never knew if they were going to get there. Life is very uncertain; they might have died before achieving their goal or just at the point when they did succeed. Yet that never stopped anyone beginning in such a training. And think, all that was just for a temporary job or position. But we are in training for eternal life. Is it likely to be easier than an earthly training? So we must expect difficulties, expect grief, expect temptation, expect setbacks. We must let all of this teach us patience. We have enlisted under a vic-

torious captain who also experienced sorrow even to death. But beyond this there is joy. We were created to live with Christ. So we allow none of the world's vanities to come between us; we live with him now, and we shall live with him in thanksgiving and praise eternally.

5) What then is the best picture of our human life, so changeable, so uncertain? Think of it as a roadway along which we travel. This life is not our home, but it is the way to our home. The traveller does not settle down on the road, and indeed as he leaves each stretch of the road behind him it becomes no more than a passing memory. The pilgrim travels with his mind fixed on the goal. He does not have false expectations about the travelling; he knows it can be rough, demanding, arduous. He thinks about the joys of getting home, but he is prepared to wait for those joys until he actually gets there.

6) So as we travel through this life we are prepared to travel light. It would be stupid to burden ourselves with 'luggage' which is not necessary, which only holds us back. It would be stupid not to realise that we cannot grasp and keep the things of this world which are constantly changing. Instead we must see this life clearly as a transient thing. We make use of it on our way towards our goal; but we must know that only on the other side of death can we see the really true and permanent things. Let's not be deceived; this life will end and then, in eternity, we shall really see and possess the truth.

7) There is much in this life that is evil and ugly, totally unworthy of our love. Yet some people love these things. Let us try to see clearly and respond appropriately: to turn away from everything corrupting, to hate what ought to be hated, to despise what ought to be despised, to reject what is filthy in any sense. People choose what will in fact enslave them and ruin their lives. But we take control; we deny ourselves evil delights and satisfactions; we are content here to accept the poverty of self-denial, for we know that we can't have both the selfish pleasure of this world and the true joys of the kingdom of heaven.

8) For, as travellers, we have a destination and we long to arrive at it. Our destination is our fatherland, and that must be where

God our Father is; our longed-for home is in heaven. Yet, though heaven is our Father's home, and there we shall see him clearly, we do in a sense see him here, enough at least to make our journey joyful. So we are happy travellers as we ponder the end of our journey. Always we must beware of the temptation to rest or pause on the way; always we must avoid the entanglements that would hold us back. Keep the vision of the end, of the beauty and joy and peace of the Father's presence, and travel with persistence and hope.

9) But is the end of the road, beyond death, to be joy and peace for everyone? No, there is judgement. We all travel through life, are born, grow, mature, decline and die. And then? Then the judgement of God will weigh up the value of each life. Brothers, it is right to fear that judgement and to ponder it, for it is real. God is very merciful and we know that we experience his mercy in this life. But we must not presume on it, for he is also just, and it is possible to lose everything: to lose the life of heaven, to lose even ourselves. What will have been the use of our lives if we lose everything in the end? So we must constantly, every day, review our lives, so that we are not diverted from our goal by the trivial pleasures of this life. The good man lives, in the best sense, both before and after death; the wicked man, after death, loses both the pleasure of his evil life here and the chance of eternal happiness there.

10) I must emphasise, my brothers, the crucial nature of this choice. Many passages in scripture warn us that God in the end cannot tolerate evil. So in this life we must make his will our will, accepting martyrdom if that should be given to us but, if not martyrdom, accepting that we die to our own will, that we choose God's way, so that Christ may live in us. I say 'choose' because we humans have free will and we can choose to give ourselves and the whole of our lives to God. But there are enemies, spiritual enemies, against all that is good. So we think of ourselves as God's 'soldiers', and soldiers do not go to sleep on the battlefield! And we think of ourselves as God's 'slaves', and no slave is free to please himself. We are to follow Christ and imitate him. But not sadly or reluctantly! We think of the goal to which we are travelling and we wonder: could any people be happier than we are?

11) God made human beings 'in his own image'. What an amazing privilege! He asks us to restore the image to him unspoilt, by the life of holiness we lead. It would be possible to allow a different image, one of evil, to be painted on us, but we must let Christ paint his image. As he does so he will give us his peace. But peace must be preserved, and here I must warn of the destructive power of the tongue. It is wise, brothers, not to let our tongues run away, but to speak carefully and not too much, for it is the easiest thing to destroy peace with the tongue, to lie, to criticise, to denigrate others, or even just to waste time and life with idle words. By our use of speech our love for others can be measured, and there is nothing more important than love; nothing deserves judgement more than the wilful destruction of it.

12) Keep the sense of being under judgement alive. Avoid lukewarmness. Imagine yourself under sentence of death; wouldn't you find enormous energy to try every possible means to escape? You are potentially under sentence of death, for there is judgement; so be watchful, be aware, shake off sloth, pray and live in constant recollection of where life is going. Ask God to live in constant recollection of where life is going. Ask God to kindle his light and his fire in our lives, so that we may be possessed by his love and live in his light and goodness.

13) Brothers, I have thought it right to speak very plainly, and not conceal the essential things of our way of life. Be thirsty and hungry for God, for he is the fountain of life and the living bread. As we eat and drink from him in this life never let us be satisfied, for he is always beyond us with more to give. And so, Lord, I pray for myself, that I too may drink of that living fountain, that I too may be wounded with love for you and know your healing, for you are my Lord and God for ever.

APPENDIX TWO: COLUMBANUS' LETTER SIX

This little piece of writing is a puzzle. The experts agree, on the grounds of style, that it is a genuine work of Columbanus. But it can not be assigned to any known date or occasion in his life. Was it a letter at all? It is written to an unnamed person and lacks the normal greeting and farewell of the letter-style. In the early manuscripts it was sometimes included with the Sermons and the Penitentials rather than with the other letters. So perhaps it belongs here, with the series of sermons.

The recipient is a young monk who has asked for further instruction in the monastic life. We know that Columbanus' community did include young men, of whom Jonas names two: Domoal and Chagnoald. But nothing more is known about these two. It could be that the 'recipient' was not a real person but a literary fiction, representing younger monks in general.

It seems clear that this piece of writing is intended to be taken away, read carefully and pondered: a piece of 'spiritual reading' in fact. The sentences are carefully constructed; the longest sentence has 72 phrases, all dependent on the opening main verb. This would be a test and perhaps a strain for anyone's listening capacity even if accustomed to oral instruction.

The letter sets out a list of the qualities of character required in the monastic life. This could easily function as a kind of check-list in self-examination, as the novice asks himself whether or where he is making improvements. He is to be a strong and vigorous fighter, so as to win all the battles in temptations coming either from his own desires or from outside. He is to be very co-operative and obedient to those in authority, showing humility wherever possible. He is to be a good friend to his contemporaries, not critical of others but generous and helpful as they grow together in the life they have all chosen.

All this is set before the novice in some detail. The letter can be compared with Columbanus' other writing to a young man, the poem *Mundus Iste Transibit* (see ch 5). But that was written, it seems, to a young man (or young men in general) who had not yet made up his mind and so the delights and rewards of the monastic life had to be set attractively before him. About the delights of heaven Letter 6 says much less than the poem. But that could be because the young monk in Letter 6 has already made his choices; he knows where he is going; he needs help to get there with as much determination as he can. So the letter encourages him to move single-mindedly along the path he has already marked out for himself, and the writer, who here is in a confident and paternal mood, will assist his journey.

CHAPTER TEN

After Columbanus: Jonas' Second Book

If Jonas had not written his second book historians would have thought the first, although a well-constructed account, unusual in at least two ways. First, he includes many more details about social and political matters than was normal in a hagiography, so, even though he was not writing 'history', his book is a useful quarry for historians seeking to trace the development of the period. Secondly, he lacks the stories of posthumous miracles which in that age were the major proof that the saint had arrived in heaven and was able to offer help and healing. So Book I ends abruptly; Book II shows that Jonas' plan was to describe the work of Columbanus' disciples and the growth of monasteries following his Rule.

To write in two books was almost though not entirely unprecedented. Of course, as a biblically-trained monk, Jonas knew that two books of the New Testament, the gospel according to Luke and the Acts of the Apostles, were by the same evangelist, that Jesus dies and rises at the end of Book I and that Book II consists of the exploits of some of the apostles. But there the similarity between Luke and Jonas ends, for Acts is a well-planned narrative leading up to a clear conclusion: it traces the progress of the gospel from the tiny provincial capital city of the Jews up to its triumphant arrival in Rome, the heart of the great Empire. By contrast Jonas' Book II has been called a 'rag-bag', lacking any clear structure which would hold it together. There is no English translation of this book (though there is a French version, *see Bibliography*). So its content will be described.

It falls into four parts:

1) The Life of Attala
He succeeded Columbanus as Abbot of Bobbio. Born a Burgundian

nobleman, after the usual education he went to Lérins but, after many years, finding that monastery not strict enough he moved to Luxeuil, then to Bobbio.

As Abbot he tried to enforce the whole of Columbanus' Rule but a group of dissidents found it too harsh and eventually broke away. But dreadful fates awaited the leaders of this group: one died of a fever, one of an axeblow, one drowned in a little stream and another in a shipwreck. A number of others returned to Attala, were well-received and were reinstated in the Bobbio community. The incident recalls that Columbanus had expressed a fear, in his fourth letter, that dissent would arise when he himself was not there to quell it, and that Attala might be too gentle.

Jonas recounts various miracles done by Attala, which he, Attala's secretary at the time, witnessed. The river Bobbio in torrent menaced the monastery's windmill, but Attala sent his staff to divert the river to the other side of the hill. On another occasion one of the monks cut off his thumb with a farm implement and Attala re-attached it with his saliva. In Milan the parents of a dying child asked Attala to heal him; Attala delayed a long time for the sake of humility but eventually did so.

Attala was given fifteen days' warning of his death. He sent Jonas to Susa to visit his (Jonas') parents, but asked him to return quickly. He did, found Attala still alive, and was able to record a vision of heaven he received the day before he died.

2) The Life of Eustasius

Eustasius became Abbot of Luxeuil when Columbanus and his companions moved on, beginning their journey to Italy. First Jonas described his intervention in the life of Burgundofara, a daughter of the nobleman Chagneric, whose son Chagnoald was already a monk. As a child she had been consecrated to the religious life by Columbanus but later her father tried to force her into marriage. When she affirmed that she did not consent to this she recovered from an illness from which she had been suffering, but when her father persisted she ran away. Eventually he was persuaded to allow her to found a monastery, Eboriacum or Faremoutiers, of which Jonas will have much more to say.

Jonas then records some of Eustasius' other successes. He does missionary work among the Warasques, converting both pagans and heretics to the Catholic faith. He performs miracles of healing, notably of a blind girl Salaberga who later in life founded several monasteries. Back at home he attracts many to 'the remedy of penance' and inspires many to become pastors of churches, of which Jonas gives a list.

But serious opposition to Eustasius was growing. Its leader was a certain Agrestius, who joined Luxeuil and while still a novice asked to be sent as a missionary to the pagans. As he could not be dissuaded he was allowed to go, failed in Bavaria, moved on to Aquilea, where he met the Three Chapters schism and joined the schismatics. He attempted to persuade both Attala in Bobbio and Eustasius in Luxeuil of the rightness of this schism but, failing to gain adherents, he then mounted an attack on the *Rule of Columbanus*. Eventually the matter went to a synod of the bishops of Burgundy at Mâcon. Here Agrestius' complaints (as represented by Jonas) seem trivial: he said that the usages of Luxeuil were against the normal practices and instanced the numerous occasions when the sign of the cross was made and the multiplication of prayers. Eustasius easily replied that there could not be too much of these good things. The result of the synod, according to Jonas, was inconclusive, but it may well be that some more important matters, such as the date of Easter, were revisited.

Agrestius continued to seek for supporters for his opposition including the Abbess Burgundofara, who repulsed him. But he did gain the temporary support of two who had previously upheld the rule, Amatus and Romaric. However, Agrestius was eventually murdered, Amatus and Romaric were reconciled to Eustasius, and the Gallic bishops supported the *Rule of Columbanus* though perhaps in a modified form.

Jonas then mentions a number of new monasteries founded under this Rule. Because of pressure of recruits, Eustasius and his successor Walbert were themselves obliged to found more houses. Eustasius died after a 30-day illness.

3) The Miracles of Eboriacum

Eboriacum (Faremoutiers) was the monastery founded by Burgundofara. Jonas does not describe the life or achievements of the foundress, possibly in order not to cause her embarrassment as she was still alive. Instead he recounts a number of deathbed scenes, mostly of good nuns, with a few bad ones included as a warning.

Two of the nuns, Sisetruda and Gibitruda, have near-death experiences. Sisetruda was told she would die in forty days, but after thirty-seven was taken to heaven by two young men in white robes only to be returned to earth for the remaining three days and then escorted by the same two young men. Gibitruda after 'death' found herself at the Judgement, but was sent back to be reconciled to three of the sisters, after which she died.

A number of the dying nuns saw light as they died, or heard music, or left a sweet perfume. One, Wilsinda, saw a company of previously dead Sisters coming for her. Another, Deurechilda, saw the Father and the Son coming for her; another, Leudeberta, was met by St Peter. Sometimes the nuns watching by the bedside were aware of music, of angels singing, or of perfume. Some of those mentioned were just children when they died: one had entered with her mother whom she persuaded to remain committed and, dying first, obtained relief from her mother's pain.

But it was not all good: two young sisters who had become disaffected with the monastic life died. They saw 'Ethiopians' coming for them, and the other sisters saw dark shadows. They were buried on the edge of the cemetery, and cries were heard at Lent and Easter at their tombs for three years.

Some of the miracles did not involve death. Some sisters who tried to escape were revealed on the ladder by a thunderstorm. A nun became so hungry that she ate in secret and after that found for a year that she could eat only herbs. Another who stole food was taken ill and nearly died.

Jonas seems to have found this monastery particularly well-supplied with this kind of story, but it is clear that all was not smooth and easy there.

4) The Life of Bertulf

Bertulf was a nobleman of barbarian family who joined the monastery at Luxeuil in the time of Eustasius. When Attala came there on a visit, Bertulf returned to Bobbio with him, and on Attala's death Bertulf was elected Abbot.

The most important event during his time was a conflict with Probus, Bishop of Tortona, who naturally thought that the monastery of Bobbio, situated within his diocese, should be under his control. Other bishops agreed with him but King Ariowald protected the monks, though refusing to intervene in religious matters. He supported Bertulf's proposal that he should consult Pope Honorius at Rome. The Pope and the Abbot got on well. Honorius saw the monastery as staunchly Catholic and therefore an ally against the Arians. Bertulf obtained a papal privilege, whereby no bishop could have authority over the monastery. This is the first known example of 'privilege', later to be used extensively, so in this respect Bobbio made history.

On his way home, Bertulf became ill, but St Peter appeared to him and cured him. Later Bertulf himself cured two demoniacs and a leper.

Jonas attached a few miscellaneous miracle stories to the end of his narrative. Two relate to the time of Attala. A priest, Blidulf, on a journey was attacked and left for dead, apparently at the instigation of the king; but when he was found he rose up quite well. A monk on a journey set fire to a pagan sanctuary; the pagans tried to throw him in to the river, even weighting him down, but the river refused to drown him and he escaped safely. Two monks saw splendid visions before they died. One monk was able to feed thirty brethren from one duck and a small piece of bread. A monk forbade a fox to eat grapes; the fox disobeyed and died. Two monks were able between them to carry a huge tree-trunk.

So Jonas ended his book, so different from Book I, and left a number of questions for scholars. For example, did Jonas write the whole of Book II? Similarities of language and style indicate that he did, so this has not been a matter of dispute. But it has been suggested that he did not intend all chapters for all readers, but that the Luxeuil section would go to Luxeuil, the Bobbio sections to

Bobbio, and the Faremoutiers (Eboriacum) chapters would go to
Faremoutiers. But the manuscript copies which survive do not
support this. Although no manuscript is currently extant which
preserves the whole of Book II in the order in which it is now
printed, the best manuscripts keep to this order for those sections
which they include. This would be very remarkable if the book
had never circulated as a whole; it is more likely that later scribes
extracted from the complete book the sections in which they were
particularly interested, and so manuscripts were produced with
sections missing. But now it is probable that we can read it as
Jonas wrote it.

It is not usually possible for an historian to check the historical
truth in a hagiography, since he has no other evidence to compare
with it. However, the survival of so much of Columbanus' genuine writing creates this opportunity and, by showing how select-
ively and 'creatively' Jonas has dealt with his subject, can reveal
something of his thinking. The most striking example of this is
given by Columbanus' second letter, to the synod of Gallic bishops, which uncovers the depth of their opposition to this foreign
infiltrator and his unacceptable Irish ideas, and uncovers also the
depth of his intransigent faithfulness to his native customs. Jonas
has no hint of this conflict. For him the opposition comes solely
from Brunhild and her royal descendants; she alone is responsible
for all Columbanus' troubles and especially for the order for his
expulsion from the kingdom, and so Jonas concentrates all his
anger on her. It is indeed very probably that it was the loss of royal
favour that required Columbanus to go in the end, but it is also
very probably that it was this same royal favour that enabled him
to stay so long – without it the opposition of the bishops would
have silenced him much earlier. Of this Jonas says nothing, presumably because it was essential to his presentation that everyone
and everything supported Columbanus until Brunhild entered as
villain. The story was, up to that point, one of growth, victory, and
even sunshine!

But in Book II Jonas describes conflict after conflict. Attala had
trouble with his own dissident monks. Eustasius had serious
trouble with the opposition led by Agrestius. The nuns of

Faremoutiers were divided between the good and the bad, and their ultimate fates differed accordingly. Bertulf had trouble with the Bishop of Tortona, and the remaining stories indicate the trouble with the Arians or pagans. It seems that Jonas had no hesitation in describing the problems that arose after Columbanus' death. So why this difference between the two books?

Jonas is balancing two obligations: he must be loyal to the memory of his hero Columbanus, and he must be realistic about his readers, who principally were the monks and nuns of the next generation for whom a number of things had changed. There can be no doubt about Columbanus' personal sanctity, the continuing devotion to him of his disciples, and the growth of monasteries talking inspiration from him. But Jonas is writing for a more peaceful age than that experienced either by the master or by his immediate followers. Jonas' readers know that there have been changes: above all they know that, at the time of Jonas' writing, the authorities of both church and state are actually supporting Columbanian monasticism.

So some changes must have occurred and among these, it may be suggested, are the acceptance by the monks of the continental dating of Easter and the modification of some of the harshness of Columbanus' original Rule. The Irish dating of Easter may well have been one of the accusations against Eustasius at the Synod of Mâcon, though Jonas does not say so and is content to mention minor charges. But it seems required that after this synod Luxeuil did alter its position about the Easter question or the bishops would never have supported it. Bobbio also must have altered its stance, perhaps at the time Bertulf went to see the Pope. The discussion between them may have been the first time that the Pope realised that Ireland had a different way of reckoning the date of Easter, for it was the same Pope Honorius who then wrote to the Irish churches urging them to conform to continental usage, as many of them did. It seems unlikely that he would have given a privilege and the commission to seek to evangelise the Arians to a monastery he considered to be itself in heresy or, at best, in disagreement.

So it is likely that the Columbanian monasteries gradually conformed about the date of Easter. It is also likely that they softened their practice by the adoption of a 'mixed Rule'. The *Rule of St Benedict* may have been known to Columbanus himself. It is well supplied with precisely what Columbanus' Rule lacked, that is, detailed instructions for the everyday life of the monastery. It could be that even in his lifetime parts of it were drawn upon in his monasteries, for it must be remembered that, at this point in the development of monasticism, written rules covering everything were not thought essential: the Abbot himself was the living Rule and he could modify his decisions as circumstances required. Later, a piece of evidence for such a 'mixed Rule' is the *Rule of Faremoutiers*, the monastery to which Eustasius sent monks to teach the monastic way. This Rule has survived: it has clear evidence that it is Columbanian but also makes much use of the Benedictine Rule. It seems that such use of a 'mixed Rule' became normal among Columbanian foundations, until the time when they became wholly Benedictine.

For those of Jonas' readers who were monks and nuns (the majority) this kind of compromise was their normal state of life, though Jonas never underlines that it has happened. For church authorities it was acceptable and enabled them to support the spread of Columbanian monasticism. For the kings and nobles also the situation at the time of Jonas' writing was acceptable. A branch of the Merovingians was now in power throughout Francia which had been friendly to Columbanus and violently hostile to Brunhild and her family: they would have had no problem in agreeing with Jonas' presentation of her.

So Jonas had written a hagiography which took account both of Columbanus' own story and of the situation prevailing some thirty years after his death. But in assessing Book II it must be remembered that he is still a hagiographer, free to give his particular 'slant' to what he records. The remarkable survival of Columbanus' letters gives the historian insight into Jonas' slant when he is writing Book I. There is (so far) no similar evidence to place alongside Book II.

So we can say goodbye to Jonas, with thanks for a remarkable piece of writings. His own life-story is a little hazy: after a few years as secretary to Attala and Bertulf, he seems to have travelled away from Bobbio, to have spent time at Luxeuil and possibly at Faremoutiers, and also to have worked as a missionary with St Amand among the northern Franks. He was back at Bobbio when Bertulf asked him to write the *Life of Columbanus*, in about 639; he dedicated it to Bertulf's successor Bobolenus and to Abbot Waldebert of Luxeuil. Jonas possibly then became an Abbot himself, at the mixed but predominantly women's community at Marchiennes.

CHAPTER ELEVEN

The spread of 'Columbanian Monasticism'

Columbanus during his lifetime had certainly known the value of the friendship of kings and had experienced more of their friendship than of their enmity. He ignored bishops, but cultivated kings and their attendant aristocracy. After his death the huge spread of monasteries owing inspiration to his original foundations, especially Luxeuil, and to his Rule and ideals, was due very largely to the Frankish kings and nobles who, in the north and east of Francia and beyond, founded a large number of these houses.

One reason for this enthusiasm appears to be social, a change in the position of the Frankish aristocracy between c.575 and c.625. For most of the sixth century the Franks had had no hereditary noble class. They had a king, and their nobles were those of their class of freemen whom he called to exercise office under him. But as they settled in the territory of the previous Roman Empire, and as they in this way became aware of a system of landowning aristocracy, the Frankish nobles began to acquire and hold land which they could pass on to their heirs, so establishing their families as powerful in a particular area of the country. Of course the kings continued to appoint powerful men to hold office but these men now had also a power base elsewhere quite apart from their office at court. A series of royal minorities and wars decreased the royal power and increased that of these nobles.

These were the people who supported 'Columbanian monasticism'. As they became Christian in more than just name they saw the advantage of having a Christian centre on their own estates. In earlier centuries in the south of the country, where the influence of the Roman Empire was still strong, most monasteries had been founded by bishops and established in the cities, but Columbanus had chosen to found his monasteries in country areas and the nobles saw the advantages of this. Such a house could be a centre for local evangelism, for teaching and for worship. But perhaps also a local monastery, founded on the estate of the local lord, could satisfy the desires of some members of the lord's family to become monks and nuns, abbots and abbesses, and enable them to do so on their own property. In the case of heiresses who became nuns this would mean that their inheritance would stay within the family rather than being alienated to a husband. By founding a monastery the aristocratic family would give a gift to their locality and also have the benefits of possessing a spiritual 'wing', particularly of women whose prayer would be a valuable support since women were vaguely supposed to be more 'spiritual' than men and in any case would not be involved in warfare or politics.

But of course there was also genuine piety in founding these houses. The Frankish nobles saw a good deal in the way of life of Columbanus and his original Irish monks which they could respect. They liked the Irish monks' radical approach, their toughness, their whole-heartedness. They could admire their competence in biblical studies, realising that they did indeed live out their ideals. Those who had met Columbanus himself and encountered his considerable personal charism as well as his total commitment seem to have been changed forever by the experience. So the story of the expansion begins with those with whom he had had this direct contact.

Some of these were just children, members of aristocratic families, when they met him. The most highly placed socially was the household of a 'duke', Waldelenus, and his wife, Flavia. They were childless and took the initiative in approaching Columbanus and asking him to pray for a child for them. He offered to pray that they would have more than one, on condition that he was allowed to baptise the first. When this child was born Columbanus named him Donatus, and at a suitable age he was brought back to Luxeuil to be educated in the monastery; later he became Bishop of Besancon and founded a monastery there. A second son, called Ramelen, succeeded his father as 'duke' and then founded a monastery in the Jura mountains, though apparently did not become a monk himself. This is one of many examples of close connections between those who held secular office at the king's court and the monastic movement. Flavia bore also two daughters, and after her husband's death founded a nunnery at Besançon, to which she gave full support and protection.

A second aristocratic family was that of Chagneric, a king's counsellor, whose eldest son, Chagnoald, was already a monk at Luxeuil and introduced Columbanus to the rest of his family. Visiting them, Columbanus blessed the young daughter, Burgundofara, who later became Abbess of the monastery of Faremoutiers. Another child, Burgundofaro, who seems to have been her brother, spent time in the king's service at his chancery and then became Bishop of Meaux. (A group was gradually being formed of bishops who were not hostile to Columbanus and his movement!) Another brother, Chagnulf, became Count of Meaux. Again we see the intertwining of the king's court and the monastic movement.

Yet another aristocratic family was that of Autharius and Aega. They had sons under the age of 10, whom Columbanus 'consecrated with his blessing'. The elder, Ado, founded the nunnery of Jouarre, where a cousin was the first Abbess. The younger, Dado, more frequently called Audoin, at first served in the king's chancery, then founded a monastery at Rebais where the first Abbot was a former monk of Luxeuil, and then became Bishop of Rousen, and encouraged the founding of other monasteries in the area of the lower Seine.

When we move outside the circle of those who actually met Columbanus the names come thick and fast. In many cases links were made of friendship rather than kinship. Many promising young aristocratic Christian men began their career with a spell of service in the king's chancery, for if the king was supportive of the monasteries his court was the best place for making connections. It was at the court of the pious king Dagobert I that Audoin, who seems to have had a genius for friendship, met Eligius, a fascinating character whose life story is worth a little space.

Eligius became the only Frankish church leader of this time who is known not to have been aristocratic. He came from Aquitaine, but nothing else is known of his family. But somehow a decision was taken for him which turned out to be supremely right: he was apprenticed to a goldsmith, to Abbo, master of the mint at Limoges. At the time such mints operated under royal licence, and the masters were people of considerable local influence. Here the people Eligius met would give him wider horizons. From there he attracted the notice of the royal treasurer and entered his service. Then the king (Clothar II) became aware of his talents and asked him to make a throne decorated with gold and jewels. Eligius actually made two thrones from the allotted amount of materials. The king was so impressed by this that he made him goldsmith-in-chief. It is possible that one or two fragments of his work survive and show him to have been a very fine artist/craftsman.

So Eligius worked at the court and came under the same roof as some of the aristocratic young men serving the king there who were going on to be important churchmen. In particular he made a significant friendship with Audoin. He was already a religious man: it was said that he studied his Bible while actually doing his metal work. He progressed in his career, becoming in turn master of the mint at Marseilles and Paris. He seems to have had diplomatic skills and was entrusted with diplomatic missions especially to the Bretons. He became wealthy through his work and used his money to ransom slaves, which was a constant preoccupation of Christians with a social conscience at the time. It was said that Eligius was able to ransom 'whole shiploads of prisoners, men and women, up to a hundred', many of them English. When they were set free he allowed them to choose their own futures. But of course, at the court, Eligius had caught the passion for Columbanian monasticism, and some of his freed people became monks and nuns.

He founded monasteries himself, at Ferrieres and Solignac. As usual the King (now Dagobert I) was involved in these foundations and gave a generous gift of land. The first Abbot of Solignac was Remaclus, a monk of Luxeuil, so showing where Eligius had discovered his spiritual home.

Eligius and Audoin both became bishops in the same year, 641. Eligius was Bishop of Noyon until his death in 660. He is said to have done good work among his flock. One of the signs of the times was that he thought it important to seek for and find the bones of the martyr Quentin, which would have increased his reputation in his diocese, as the cult of relics was becoming popular.

His *Vita* was written by his friend Audoin, and his life story indicates that it was not impossible among the Franks for someone humbly born to attain pre-eminence if he had the talent. His life is one more example of the importance of the palace in the life of the church.

Another story to show the involvement of the royal court in the life of the church is that of a woman, Balthild, and it has more than a touch of fairytale. She is first encountered as a slavegirl in the household of the Frankish nobleman, Erchinoald. She was English. How she became enslaved is not known, though there was a considerable slavetrade between the Anglo-Saxons and the Franks; sometimes slaves were captives from war. They might of course have been of high social position at home before they were taken captive.

Balthild was beautiful and her master, on the death of his wife, wished to marry her. She is said to have disguised herself and hidden away until he had married someone else. Then, somehow, King Clovis II noticed her; she married him, and so the slavegirl became Queen. She ruled with her husband until his death in 657 and then, for about seven years, she ruled alone as regent for her son until he came of age. The policies which make her notable belong to this period. Our information comes from a *Vita*, written probably by a nun of the community of Chelles where she spent her last years. This document naturally has a strong ecclesiastical bias.

Balthild was passionately interested in the spread of monasticism. She founded monasteries, of which the best-known are Corbie, Jumieges and Chelles: the latter may have been a refoundation of a previous house, and seems to have been her favourite, for she chose it for her own retirement and death. Founding a monastery, of course, gave her a voice in the appointment of the Abbot or Abbess and her appointments showed she was strongly 'Columbanian': at Corbie the first Abbot and monks were from Luxeuil, and for Chelles she brought an Abbess and nuns from Jouarre, which had been founded by Ado, who had been 'consecrated' as a child by Columbanus.

Balthild as Regent had considerable influence in the appointment of bishops and chose those sympathetic to the monastic movement: Audoin in particular was her friend and supporter. She also tried to rid the church of the immoral practice of simony (the purchase of ecclesiastical office). This apparently had previous been rife, and Balthild completely forbade it.

At a time when the cult of relics was burgeoning and the shrines of saints growing in popular importance Balthild did all she could to encourage the care of these, which would add greatly to the power and prestige of the bishop among the local people. She also took the step of converting some of the major shrines into monastic centres if they were not already staffed by monks. Here she used freely her power to grant immunities: that is, to remove these shrines and monasteries from the oversight of the diocesan bishop, to guarantee the monks freedom to choose their own abbots and to own their monastic property, while at the same time requiring that the bishop would be available to ordain their priests and consecrate their altars. In return, of course, the monastery guaranteed a continual ministry of prayer and intercession, especially for the lives and work of their benefactors. These new monasteries were modelled on the life and practices of Luxeuil.

All this was not achieved without opposition, for some bishops in particular objected that the old ways were being undermined, involving the loss of considerable revenue to the diocese. Consequently the scandal-mongers of the time attacked Balthild, accusing her of complicity in the death of Aunemundus, Bishop of Lyons, and of eight other unnamed bishops. But the evidence, of course, is totally lacking.

Nonetheless it is possible that there was an element of compulsion in her retirement from power and the handing over of the kingdom to her son, Clothar III. She went to her own monastery of Chelles, to live there in obedience to the Abbess whom she herself had appointed, to take a full part in the menial work of the monastery, to pray and eventually to die with a reputation of sainthood among those who knew her in her last years. Hers was a truly remarkable life.

Many other names could be mentioned of those who founded monasteries and those who encouraged their foundation. Very frequently indeed, where we can trace it, the thread of connection leads back to Luxeuil. Its monks are found everywhere in this rapidly spreading movement. Luxeuil became a 'nursery for bishops' as Lérins had been at an earlier time, and as its bishops went out they took with them something of the spirit and influence of Columbanus.

According to his correspondence, Columbanus at one time considered the idea of missionary work that is, of deliberate movement into pagan territory. But he did not follow this up himself, apart from taking opportunities to spread the gospel where pagans crossed his path. Of course, how much work was done by and from his monasteries to people still pagan who lived in the area cannot be known. But his own heart seems to have been in the life of his own houses. However, his successor at Luxeuil, the Abbot Eustasius, was actively missionary minded: he promoted mission by working himself among a local people called the Warasci, and then leading a mission to the Bavarians. Jonas described in detail (see ch 10) Eustasius' opposition to the demand of a certain Agrestius to be sent as a missionary to the Bavarians, judging him to be immature in the monastic life; when Agrestius in the end went on this mission he was a failure.

The principal missionary associated with the 'Columbanian movement' was Amandus. The outline of his life can be traced, though some details are hazy. He was born about the year 590, that is, about the time Columbanus came from Ireland to the continent of Europe. His family were well-to-do and lived somewhere near the lower part of the river Loire; he was given a good education appropriate to his class. He seems to have taken himself, as a youth, to join the monastery on the tiny island of Yeu, not far from the port of Nantes, and to have resisted his father's attempt to persuade him to rejoin secular life. He journeyed to Tours and at the shrine of St Martin vowed himself to a life of *peregrinatio*, never to return home. Then he journeyed to the city of

Bourges and, with the support of the bishop, became a hermit for some years living in a cell in the city walls. He then visited Rome, met the Pope, possibly discussed missionary activity, and then had a mystical encounter with St Peter, who told him to return to Gaul and become an evangelist. When he did return he was persuaded, at the insistence of the king (possibly Clothar II), to become a bishop though not attached to any particular place.

The king with whom he worked most closely was Dagobert I, already mentioned as very keen on the expansion of the mission of the church and of the monastic movement. At the time, the Frankish royal power was being extended to the north and east. Amandus, by the king's gift of land, founded a monastery at Elnone which was the centre of his missionary work for some time.

It is conjectured that Amandus would have known and admired the Columbanian movement for some time. There is no evidence that he actually met Columbanus, but in his youth at Yeu he would almost certainly have heard of the failed attempt to expel Columbanus from Nantes at the mouth of the Loire; perhaps he would have heard also of the episode of Columbanus' prayer at the shrine of St Martin. The diocese of Bourges, from 620 onwards, saw the foundation of several Columbanian monasteries. Amandus as a missionary seems to have turned to the Columbanian family of houses for assistance; most notably he was joined for a few years by Jonas of Bobbio, who would become Columbanus' hagiographer. Amandus also obtained some recruits by buying boys from slavery, probably Anglo-Saxons, and training them to become church leaders, as Aidan did in Northumbria. So he worked in this area to the north of Gaul, and eventually took Maastricht as a centre for his diocese.

More debatably (to us) he asked King Dagobert to use force on those of his potential converts who were not willing to receive baptism. In this he was not out of step with other missionaries of this time and later. Baptism was not then considered to be the final step, to be accepted after a considerable amount of Christian teaching had prepared potential converts to make the decision for themselves. Rather, it was administered near the beginning of the conversion process. The thinking behind this was that baptism would transfer the convert from the sphere of the devil into the sphere of God, in which more detailed teaching about the Christian faith and life would be suitable. We have no information about any methods used by Dagobert for forcible conversion and often it was not needed: the example of the upper classes was sufficient.

Amandus worked in other places apart from the area of Maastricht. He founded monasteries at Elnone, at Barisis near Soissons, and at Nant in the south of the country not far from Arles. Perhaps this last monastery was intended as a stepping stone to a mission among the Basques in the Pyrenees, which he certainly attempted but it seems without success. Another attempt, also unsuccessful, was among the Slavs. The kings supported these efforts and probably hoped to extend their kingdoms in these directions, but in this the kings were not successful. It is of course impossible to separate 'religious' and 'political' ambitions in the minds of these kings. Kings were genuinely both. But Amandus seems to have sown the idea of thrusting, adventurous missionary activity, going outside the boundaries of the former Roman Empire, which was possibly not a very familiar idea to most of his contemporaries.

Did the influence of Columbanian monasticism reach England? The background to this question is the evidence we have of contacts between the Franks of northern Gaul and the Anglo-Saxons of eastern and south-eastern England. It is a well-known fact that Ethelbert, the king of Kent who allowed St Augustine and the rest of the mission from Gregory the Great to settle there, was at the time married to a Frankish princess, Bertha. She was a daughter of King Charibert, was herself a Christian and had brought with her a bishop, Luidhard, as her chaplain. So Christianity would already have been known at the Kentish court before Augustine arrived and perhaps Ethelbert was already favourably disposed to it. His marriage also indicates that there could be political arrangements between a king of Kent and a Frankish king. It is likely that Bertha married a little below her own status, as the powerful kings of the Franks would probably not regard a king of little Kent as an equal; possibly they looked upon themselves as overlords. They retained friendship with Bertha and her family, and when her daughter Ethelburga returned to Kent from Northumbria after the death of her husband King Edwin in battle it seemed natural to send the two little boys of this family over to the Frankish King Dagobert I for safety. Ethelbert's son Eadbald, the next King of Kent, was able to marry a Frankish noblewoman but not a princess, and that may show their relative position in society.

Kent was the nearest English kingdom to Francia but East Anglia was not far away. We know that an East Anglian prince, Sigwald, whose name suggests he might have had Frankish connections, had gone to Gaul when he had to flee from the threats of King Raedwald of East Anglia. A further connection is indicated by the fact that a hoard of coins found at the burial place at Sutton Hoo probably came from the Franks in the early 7th century. By this time the Frankish aristocracy, who had long since adopted the Christian faith in its Catholic form, were among Columbanus' main disciples, so it is by no means impossible that their enthusiasm would have spread to England.

The clearest evidence would have been documentary, i.e. evidence that Columbanus' writings, especially his Rules, were known in England. But there is no such evidence, and perhaps it should not be expected, in view of the fact that monasticism was still in its early experimental phase. There were no Religious Orders; each monastery was a separate foundation and not all the Abbots and Abbesses, who held the ultimate authority, chose to write their arrangements and decisions in the form of a Rule. Even those who did so, most famously St Benedict of Nursia, wrote their Rule with just their own one monastery in mind, and had no expectation that it would be transferred *en bloc* to other places. Abbots and Abbesses certainly consulted other Rules where they could get them, but then made their own selection.

So the best evidence for the movement of ideas and their influence will be in the movement of the people who could have carried these ideas. We can identify several of these people.

First, there were the English people who travelled through Gaul, who must have met there the monasteries of the north, and who then returned to England to spread the monastic movement here. An example is Benedict Biscop, the founder of Wearmouth-Jarrow, who contented himself with founding just one monastery but deliberately organised it according to the best features of the many monasteries he had visited on the continent. Compared with Lindisfarne, Wearmouth-Jarrow had a Benedictine feel, but it would be an anachronism to describe it as 'Benedictine'. Another example of a person who travelled extensively in and through Gaul and elsewhere on the continent is St Wilfrid, who returned to England to found many monasteries based on his experiences. But his houses lived by their founder's own arrangements not by the *Rule of St Benedict*. Since Wilfrid had spent a considerable amount of time in Lyons he could hardly have missed the Columbanian monasteries.

Secondly, we can name people who originated in Gaul but then were appointed to positions in the English church. One of the most intriguing is Bishop Agilbert, who had studied for a time in Ireland, became a bishop in England (without much knowledge of English), was present at the Synod of Whitby supporting the continental side of that argument, and eventually withdrew back to his native Gaul. Such a well-travelled man, wherever he stayed, would surely be eagerly asked for his news. Would it be at all likely that he stayed at St Hild's Whitby without talking about the experiences of the churches on the continent?

Thirdly, there were the English ladies. Bede explains that before there were religious houses in England which could accommodate nuns, those among the English ladies who wished to take the veil had to travel over to Gaul to the Frankish houses there. He names the houses at Brie, Chelles and Andelys-sur-Seine (all these were influenced by the Columbanian tradition) and there were several others. The story of the Northumbrian noblewoman Hild will illustrate the point. She was the great-niece of King Edwin of Northumbria and was converted by the mission of Paulinus who travelled north from Canterbury; she was baptised at the age of 13. We next hear of her aged 33, when she had decided to become a nun. Her elder sister Hereswith, now widowed after a marriage into the royal house of East Anglia, had joined the monastery at Chelles. Hild proposed to follow her and, as a stage on her way, stayed with the East Anglian royal family. But Aidan, an Irish monk from Iona, had begun his mission to the Northumbrian people. He persuaded Hild to stay in her native country, to be trained in the monastic life by him, and then to become a Mother Foundress, as she did at Hartlepool and Whitby.

Did these monasteries owe nothing to the Columbanian tradition? This can be answered in part by considering what was happening further south, in East Anglia and in Kent, the kingdoms nearest to Frankish Gaul.

The King of East Anglia at the time of Hild's visit was named Anna. The activities of the women of his family show how prominent were royal ladies in the foundation of the first generation of monasteries among the Anglo-Saxons. One of his daughters founded Ely, another Sheppey, another East Dereham, another went to Gaul to become eventually the Abbess of Faremoutier, another daughter and a step-daughter became nuns at Faremoutier; a granddaughter of Anna became Abbess of Ely and a great-granddaughter was a nun and possibly Abbess of Ely. Clearly in that family Hild would find every encouragement to pursue her vocation even though she eventually pursued it at home in Northumbria. If we look at the royal house of Kent we find there also a ferment of activity: Ethelberga, daughter of King Ethelbert founded Lyming; his granddaughter founded Folkstone, his great-granddaughter Minster-in-Thanet, and a great-great-granddaughter founded Much Wenlock. We find similar activity in Wessex with the ladies of Barking and Wimbourne.

Many of these were double houses, that is, monks and nuns together in the same foundation, though of course with separate accommodation. The double houses seem to have originated in Gaul and spread from there to England. It is suggested that these houses were basically for nuns, who needed men as priests for sacramental purposes and also as workmen to maintain the buildings and gardens: and then, where there were opportunities for learning as at Hild's Whitby, these houses took men as students also, and trained them for the priesthood. In Gaul most of the double houses were headed by Abbesses; in England all the double houses without exception were under the rule of Abbesses.

We may ask why, in those early years of Christianity among both the Franks and the Anglo-Saxons, were women so prominent? For it did not last. An answer suggested by the historian Patrick Wormald is that in these societies the absorption in fighting and in military virtues by the noblemen, in which women were not involved, created a gap in church life which was then filled by the women. For such men, though sincerely Christian, might have found the life of monks, of study and scholarship, to be a little 'unmanly'. He further suggests that the men were more likely to be socially conservative, maintaining their customs, where the women were free to be more innovative; in religion it was quite possible for women to take the initiative as they were considered more 'spiritual'. This 'window of opportunity' for women did not last, for as the Christian church became more embedded in society, more established, so the men took it over and the days of the great Abbesses were finished.

What Columbanus would have thought about all this we do not know. At least we know that he encouraged women to adopt the monastic life, for he 'consecrated' the child Burgundofara. But a useful bit of written evidence about the influence of the Frankish monasteries in England, and the Frankish influence on all this growth can be found in the *Vita* of Bertilla, Abbess of Chelles. Originally she was a nun of the house of Jouarre which had been founded by Ado, who was 'consecrated' as a child by Columbanus. She was moved to Chelles to be its Abbess by Queen Balthild when she reconstituted that monastery. The writer of Bertilla's *Vita* emphasises her supreme virtue as a practitioner of the Rule, a model of monastic living. We read in this *Vita* of both men and women hastening to Bertilla 'even from across the seas' and then that some of the 'faithful kings of the Saxons' asked her to send some of her disciples 'that they might build convents of men and nuns in their land'. She did: she sent many volumes of books and chosen women and devout men, though exactly where they went among the Saxons is not noted. But it reinforces the impression that the same ferment of activity was happening both sides of the channel, and that 'Columbanian monasticism' was central to it.

Many historians have pointed out that the work of spreading

Columbanian influence among the Franks was done by the Franks themselves, especially by their noblemen, and, after the initial inspiration and impulse, was not directly affected by the Irish. It seems that those Irish monks who remained from Columbanus' original group, and further Irishmen who had joined him in Gaul, were among those who left Francia with him and travelled to Bobbio. The king had forbidden Franks to accompany him, though this prohibition lasted only as long as the life of that king. Now it is time to look again at Bobbio, which it is claimed remained for a few centuries the most Irish of Columbanus' foundations.

CHAPTER TWELVE

After Jonas: Bobbio

This chapter is very much indebted to a recent book by Michael Richter, *Bobbio in the Early Middle Ages* (Four Courts Press, 2008). He comments that many continental scholars have believed that Bobbio quickly ceased to have any Irish features or connections: that it soon became an Italian monastery. His own researches have shown that many details in the three centuries after its foundation indicate a lively and continuing contact with Ireland. In view of the fact that it is generally agreed (see ch 11) that the Franks, not the Irish, were responsible for the spread of 'Columbanian monasticism' in and around Francia it will be good to note the evidence for the continuing Irishness of Bobbio as we trace the outline of its story.

Jonas' second book described some of the ecclesiastical happenings under the two Abbots of Bobbio who followed Columbanus: Attala and Bertulf. But he does not emphasise a political fact of great importance, the support that Bobbio received from the Lombard kings. Jonas has narrated that Columbanus, on entering Lombardy, went to the king's court, was kindly received and eventually was granted by King Agilulf the site of Bobbio. Supporting evidence for this is available, in that the document detailing this grant has survived. The king issued a 'precept' giving Columbanus the basilica of St Peter at Bobbio with the surrounding land.

Columbanus' successors had the political good sense to build on this royal relationship. During Attala's abbacy the next king, Adaloald, came in person to Bobbio, confirmed the grant and added further land. When Bertulf became Abbot the same king confirmed the grant to him, and the next king, Ariold supported Bertulf's visit to the Pope which resulted in the first known charter exempting a monastery from episcopal control (see ch 10).

The next Abbot was Bobulenus to whom, with the Abbot of Luxeuil, Jonas dedicated his book but whose life he does not describe. He was a Frank, had been taught by Columbanus personally, and was Abbot c.643-c.654. He quickly asked the king for confirmation of the grant and of the monks' freedom to choose their own Abbot, which was granted; he also approached the Pope and received from him confirmation of the monastery's exemption. This threefold relationship, the monastery/the king/the pope, was a source of great strength in the early decades of Bobbio's life. It seems that Bobulenus was a strong and energetic Abbot. There is one interesting further source about him: a poem in his praise found in two Bobbio manuscripts which date from the 10th century, though the poem itself was probably written soon after his death. Various details suggest it was written in Ireland, such as the poet's familiarity with an Irish hymn written in praise of St Patrick and the fact that the pattern of the poem is Irish-Latin rather than Italian-Latin. So this poem is an indication of a continuing connection with Ireland.

About the next Abbot little is known. His name apparently was Camogallus, which could easily be a variant on the Irish name Comgall, the name of Columbanus' first Abbot, the founder of Bangor. Perhaps Camogallus was Irish himself, but at least a continuing Irish connection is suggested. This is underlined by the discovery at Bobbio of a small reliquary, a 'twin' to one found in Co Antrim, Ireland; it is thought they were from the same Irish workshop and date from the 7th century. We do not know how one of them travelled to Bobbio, how it was used there, what relics it held, but again its existence indicates some kind of link with Ireland.

So it seems that Bobbio, during its first half-century, experienced peace, stability and some expansion.

Vital, of course, to any monastery at this time was its *scriptorium* and its library. We can't know what books Columbanus brought with him to Bobbio but we can be sure that his monks were all literate and that some would be good scribes, capable of producing manuscripts. In time the monastic library at Bobbio came to be very rich in manuscripts, many of which have survived to the present in libraries in Turin, Milan, the Vatican and other places. But the problems in dating a manuscript and in assigning to it a place of origin can be great and cause considerable disagreement among scholars.

First, the nature of the parchment itself can be examined. Parchment was not produced everywhere in exactly the same way, and it was characteristic of Irish parchment to be thicker than the continental type. This was one characteristic of *The Antiphonary of Bangor* which led experts to think that this little book, found at Bobbio, had travelled from Ireland (see ch 3). Also there was a characteristic Irish script, for many different ways of shaping letters had developed in different places. But Michael Richter focuses on two other features which indicate Irish scribes.

First, variations from the normal way of spelling Latin. Richter gives as an example a persistent tendency of the Irish to confuse the double ss and the single s. Latin words use both but with precision, as the wrong choice might alter the grammatical meaning. But Irish scribes often wrote the double ss instead of the single s, so that the scholar, reading this, would be alerted by this fact alone. But it might only apply to the earliest copies, as a later scribe, detecting it, would tend to correct it.

Secondly, there was a characteristic Irish set of abbreviations. All scribes came to adopt a convention of abbreviations: among other things they saved precious space on the parchment. But the reader had to be able to interpret them. Scholarly argument has turned on whether they were invented in Ireland or at an Irish centre on the continent, of which Bobbio is the most likely. In Italy they were used only in Bobbio, but they were used also in Ireland, so again contacts are indicated. The earliest Irish document to use them is *The Antiphonary of Bangor* which dates from the late 7th century.

Art historians have detected resemblances in decoration between manuscripts produced in Ireland and those produced at Bobbio in the 7th century. It is important to realise that people travelled, and perhaps the best explanation of these resemblances is that they occur on manuscripts written in Irish script at Bobbio by Irish monks newly arrived.

Mention should also be made of the 'Irish glosses'. A gloss is a comment by a scribe on a text, usually written in the margin. Such glosses, written in Irish on the margin of a Latin text, are a major source for the present study of the language now called 'Old Irish'. Again this is territory for scholars only; it seems that the present opinion of scholars is that although a fair number of texts with Old Irish glosses existed at Bobbio they were probably written in Ireland. So we do not know whether there were many Irish writers in Bobbio, but the arrival of these glossed scripts from Ireland suggest that there were Irish readers there as late as the ninth century, the date of many of these scripts.

Of course, in dealing with manuscripts, we can only argue from what has survived, and can only imagine what has not.

After the time of Abbot Camogallus, in the mid 7th century, the monastery at Bobbio enters a time of darkness in the sense that there are few records. No abbot can be named before Anastasius in 747. The darkness however is broken by two pieces of evidence.

The first is a poem composed by a Stefanus M, to be dated in the last years of the 7th century. Its subject is the synod held at Pavia in 698 at the command of King Cunicpert, in which the delegates from Aquileia abandoned their opposition to the Pope (the Three Chapters Schism, see ch 9) and the church was reunited. The poem praises the efforts of the king in particular. It is interesting in that it shows the influence of Irish-Latin poetry, not Italian-Latin poetry, and for this reason was thought by some to be rough and uncivilised, for the conventions of writing poetry were different. But, again, this shows continuing Irish influence.

The other evidence is a marble slab commemorating an Irish bishop named Cumian who came to Bobbio at the age of 78 and died there 17 years later at the age of 95. Nothing further is known of this Grand Old Man, but surely he did not come by accident – we may suppose that he knew that there was an Irish monastery at Bobbio. The inscription on his grave slab states that he came from Ireland and that he had lived under the *Rule of Columbanus*; that the monastery gave him a beautiful tomb suggests that he was a welcome and treasured guest.

During this dark period the friendship with the kings contin-

ued and charters, which have not survived, were issued by the
kings. In 747 a charter to Abbot Anastasius is extant, which deals
with a dispute between Bobbio and another monastery, situated
too close for comfort, which had apparently taken some of
Bobbio's property which was then restored.

Meanwhile in Europe an important change happened in this
eighth century: the Merovingian monarchs were replaced by the
Carolingians, still Franks but of a different family, of whom the
emperor Charles the Great, known to history as Charlemagne, is
the most outstanding. In 774 he had become by conquest King of
Lombardy also and so Bobbio was now within his realm. The
same year he gave a very substantial gift of land to the monastery,
which included forest (necessary for timber and for the all-
important pigs), arable land for cereals, grassland for animals and
for hay, small vineyards and an olive plantation for the production of olive oil. It was a very generous grant, though it was the
only one from that monarch. But Charles' son Louis granted an
immunity, as did the next monarch. At this time though the close-
ness of the relationship between the king and the monastery may
have began to work to the latter's disadvantage for it seems that
the kings began to be involved in the appointment of the abbot,
jeopardising the community's claim to complete independence.
The last major royal donation to Bobbio appears to have been that
of Charlemagne's grandson Lothar in 843. His son Louis II issued
a charter in 860 which did not grant any additional land but confirmed all the possessions and privileges of the monastery. These
included a number of donations to Bobbio by bishops, priests,
monks and laypeople, some of which had involved disputes
which had to be settled in court. Later documents suggest a divis-
ion of property between the Abbot and the monks, but it is not
known why this was necessary, who benefited and how the ar-
rangement worked, if indeed it was ever put into practice. It is
clear that there was considerable interest in the monastery on the
part of the Carolingians, especially Louis II, who of all these rulers
seems to have been most concerned about his possessions in Italy;
after his death in 875 life became more difficult for Bobbio.

One particularly interesting donation to Bobbio during this

time is from a non-royal and shows a link between the monastery
and Ireland. Donatus, Bishop of Fiesole, describing himself as an
Irishman, gave to Bobbio a church in Piacenza dedicated to St
Brigit (surely an unusual dedication for an Italian church; did he
choose the saint himself?), to provide a refuge or hospice for Irish
pilgrims, up to three in number at any time. Four or five monks
from Bobbio were to live there to maintain the church and the
house; the rest of the income went to Bobbio itself. Other donations show connections at some distance from Bobbio, with
churches or altars dedicated to St Columbanus north of the Alps.
Perhaps this shows the growth of his cult during this time.

But of course a wealthy monastery would always have enemies.
Court cases about the ownership of property arose as a result of
this hostility. The nearest monastery to Bobbio was Mezzano,
which had already been in dispute in 747 and then, a hundred
later in 847, made another attempt, claiming ownership of a property at Barbarino. But Bobbio was able to produce evidence of its
ownership, both written and spoken by local people who had long
memories. Mezzano had no such evidence so the case was decided
for Bobbio. Another kind of court case happened when a gift to the
monastery was later disputed by the donor's family, but again the
court decided for Bobbio. This is the kind of situation about which
we should like to know more, as it brings the period and its details
alive and shows us the monastery as a living, working community,
having to cope with practical but sometimes distasteful realities of
life.

The reader may wonder about practical details of life at
Bobbio. What did the monastery look like? But it is not at all easy
to know. Columbanus' earlier monasteries in Francia might have
given some clues, but they have not yet been excavated or sufficiently studied, nor has the site at Bobbio been sufficiently studied. Jonas, who lived there as a young monk, gives only the merest
hints. The original grant from the king was a piece of land, with
boundaries, enclosing a church of St Peter in disrepair, and one of
the earliest jobs was to repair it. That church presumably would
have been built in stone, though to repair it the monks cut down
wood, possibly for the roof. Jonas says that Attala lived in a cell

with a free-standing cross outside it. If both the cell and the cross
were made of wood this would have recalled the Irish monasteries where such crosses were a feature, later of stone but at first of
wood. We presume that the monks lived in wooden cells. If there
was a *scriptorium* from the very early days this would have required a somewhat larger building which might have functioned
also as the library.

We are never told the number of monks, either at the beginning or later, but we can suppose the community grew signifi-
cantly to deal with its ever growing property.

But for clearer ideas we have to wait till the 9th century when
Wala, Abbot of Bobbio 833-835, has left a written description of
the monastery. This included a list of the estates but these are
hardly more than just names. But Wala gives a picture of the various offices in the community filled either by the monks or by lay
people employed by them. There was a librarian, for by this time
there was library of several hundred scripts. There was keeper of
muniments i.e. the official documents of the house. A cellarer saw
to the provision of food for the kitchen and the refectory. Visitors
needed some kind of guestmaster, and there was probably a
building to accommodate guests. There were two infirmarians.

It seems likely that all these officials would have been monks.
But there were also craftsmen who made the clothes and the
shoes, a carpenter who would have needed workshops, and a
master gardener. A second church had been built and dedicated
to St Ambrose. If all these people lived on the site, the lay people
perhaps just outside the walls of the enclosure, the monastery
would have begun to look like a small town. Back in Ireland some
of the major monasteries had developed into large towns.

From later in the 9th century there are documents that give a
better idea of how the monastery managed its (by that time) huge
amount of property. It had to employ a lot of labourers, apparently
consisting of free men, who were under contract to the monastery,
and unfree tenants. For those who had contracts these were written documents, in two copies, one for the tenant and one for the
monastery. From surviving contracts we can see that the 'rent'
was paid partly in coin but very largely in goods. The tenant

would supply a fixed amount of grain, a number of hens and eggs, a few coins and a few days' unpaid work, often in hay production. It seems that the tenant's rent was normally a quarter of the total year's yield and the rest was his own. It is a little puzzling that there is no mention of cows, horses and donkeys, though they must have existed to eat the large quantity of hay produced; nor is there mention of sheep, though they would be required for making parchment among other things.

This information can be gathered from the contracts. But in 862 a document was drawn up covering all the monastic possessions in a systematic survey. 56 properties are listed, mainly worked by tenants. The monastery by this time had 36 buildings, most of them connected with its economic life. Some of the estates were very small, and it is noted that some wine was produced and that woodlands were important mainly because pigs were kept in them.

In 883 a second, very similar survey was produced, showing a slight increase of products of most kinds.

In general it is clear that Bobbio had become a great monastic landowner. The workforce on all the estates together was 695 males, so with their families about 3500 people. This figure does not include the monks themselves, or the slaves about whom we hear nothing and so can know nothing. The crops obtained were: from the woodlands timber and pasture for pigs, also chestnuts from a few managed estates; from grassland hay and grazing the rest of the year though the animals are not mentioned; from the arable land cereals, though which is not known, for human consumption and possibly also for making beer (the Irish favourite drink though no doubt the Italians preferred wine); vineyards. Salt was also a necessity, but the original grant had included part of a salt-pan. Oil was produced in some places.

The impression is that the monastery was self-sufficient and had no shortage of resources.

Towards the end of the ninth century, under Abbot Agilulf (c.883-896), Bobbio seems to have reached the height of its wealth and influence. Already there were political clouds on the horizon, portents of what was to come. The kings continued to be friendly and to issue charters confirming the possessions and rights of the monastery. But after the death of Louis II in 875, the last Carolingian emperor in Italy, there was a succession of comparatively short-lived and comparatively powerless kings. The amount of actual help they could give in time of trouble was to be doubted. As well as political instability, there was potential trouble between the local bishop, of Placenza, and the monastery. For example, a papal bull issued to this bishop at his request in 891 confirms his right to certain dues from the monastery, which contradicts the original papal exemption from all interference from outside, given to Abbot Bertulf.

In spite of this worrying background, Abbot Agilulf was notable for success in two areas. He is credited with a reconstruction of the main monastic church, the basilica dedicated to St Peter which was part of the original grant to Columbanus. The new altar of the reconstructed church was dedicated as before to St Peter; the building was enlarged and, particularly interesting, a crypt was constructed to hold the remains of the first three Abbots: Columbanus, Attala and Bertulf. We assume that Columbanus' original grave was outside but within the monastic enclose, and we do not know where Attala and Bertulf were first buried. In the new crypt they were placed by the north and the south walls, with the new site for Columbanus' relics in the centre. The church was beautifully decorated in marble and remains of it still survive.

Agilulf's other achievement was the provision of illuminated manuscripts for the monastic library. Some of these contain a poem referring directly to Agilulf in which he offers them as a gift to Christ. None of these are included in the library's ninth-century list of books so it is likely that they were added after his death. One of them is also the first of a group of ten manuscripts with a new style of sumptuous illustrations, no longer reflecting the Irish influence. The production of these is believed to have begun under Agilulf and shows Bobbio as a centre of the craft of illumination. It is likely that some of these illuminators were professionals, not themselves monks, but hired by the monastery to do this work, which indicates not only the wealth of the monastery but also its connections with the outside world. The Abbot must have been instrumental in achieving all this.

Apart from these remarkable additions, the library at Bobbio seems to have reached its height in terms of the number and quality of its manuscripts by the end of the ninth century. Clearly it was a notable collection and drew scholars to study there.

How far is it possible to know what books were in an early medieval monastic library which has long since been dispersed? One method is that used in an recent attempt to compile a list of the early eighth century library at Iona. This analyses carefully all the material believed to have been written on Iona up to that date to see what books were quoted or referred to by the Iona writers. But at Bobbio the starting-point is an actual list compiled, presumably by the monk-librarian, probably before 896: that date is believed to be that of the death of Abbot Agilulf and the books that he bequeathed to the library are not on the list. This list has not itself survived, but copies were made before its disappearance and have been used by modern scholars.

In the early days of the monastery the books seem to have been kept in chests labelled with the Abbot's name, possibly the name of the Abbot in whose time the books were acquired: 'from the chest of lord Attala', 'a book from the chest of lord Bobulenus'. But by the late ninth century it seems that the books were classified in part according to type. The collection has two sections: before and after the donations of an Irishman, Dungal, from about the year 825.

Surprisingly the library seems to have contained little about Columbanus, though it did have a copy of Jonas and a copy of Columbanus' Rule. It has the *Rule of Basil* but apparently no copies at all of the Benedictine Rule, which has led to the speculation that, unlike Columbanus' Frankish monasteries which seem to have adopted a mixed Rule soon after his death, Bobbio perhaps attempted to live by Columbanus' Rule alone. The list cites a good number of the Christian Latin Fathers and surprisingly a good list of Latin Classical authors. Irish writers had never shown interest in classical Rome but, after all, Bobbio was in Italy. There were books on the reckoning of dates and times, though no Bede's classic work on this subject. There were some books on canon law; not a great deal on the scriptures; a large number of books on grammar. This last fact reminds us that the Irish were the first people in Europe to learn Latin completely as a foreign language and as a sacred language. How they did it we are not clear, since the books about Latin grammar were themselves written in Latin: a competent teacher presumably would have been essential. One of these grammar books should be specially mentioned, known as the *Ars Ambrosiana*, because it is believed to have been written at Bobbio by an Irishman, using sources available in the Bobbio library and incorporating a gloss in the Old Irish language. It suggests continuing contacts between Ireland and Bobbio about the year 700.

How did all these books come into the possession of the library? Very many were individual donations and the donors are named. Others perhaps were gifts from other monasteries, for it was common practice, when a monastery received a new text, for it to make several copies, keep one or more, and give the rest as presents to honoured guests or to other monastic houses. Some books may well have come from Ireland in the luggage of Irish travelling monks.

Although we regret the loss of the librarian's catalogue of c.890 enough evidence survived to show that this library was the treasured possession of a community with wide interests and contacts, which still, at that date, had the resources to continue to add to it.

But the political situation worsened after the death of Louis II in 875. He was the last Carolingian Emperor in Italy and then, without strong rulers, the local aristocracy increased in power. These aristocrats took what they could steal and hold of the monastery's lands and possessions. So without any effective protection, the monastery's income and status declined. But the monks had 'the jewel in the crown': they still had their patron saint. The help of Columbanus might be effective where earthly help had failed. At least it could be tried.

In 929 the monastery took a dramatic step in the effort to halt its decline and recover some of the property which had been filched from it by the rapacious nobles of the area. Abbot Gerlannus decided to exhume the remains of St Columbanus and take them in procession to Pavia, hoping and expecting that the miracles performed by the saint there and on the journey would change the minds of these aristocratic thieves. We owe the details of this story to the anonymous monk of Bobbio who wrote *Miracula Sancti Columbani* mentioned in ch 9.

Abbot Gerlannus was a man of much administrative experience in the secular world, since he had earlier been the King's Chancellor; he was therefore also very familiar with the royal court. He did not immediately tell the rest of the monks of his plans, but ordered a casket to be made to hold the remains; then the work of uncovering the body began. This was difficult at first as the grave had been covered with layers of stones which refused to move until the Abbot had told St Columbanus what he intended to do. Then the community was told what was to happen. The skeleton was uncovered and the bones placed carefully in the casket. The monks gathered with candles, lights and incense. Two priests were to walk in front, carrying handbells. The people, including laypeople, followed them carrying crosses, candles and incense. Then, in the procession, came those carrying relics in the sense of objects the saint had used: his cup and his leather satchel. (This detail, together with the handbells, take us back to Ireland of centuries before. The Irish were slow to join in the cult of relics in the sense of parts of the saint's body. They preferred objects which the living saint had touched. On Iona, when Columba was buried, no special attention was paid to his grave, but objects such as his tunic, his pen and any book he had written were revered and carried in procession.) The Abbot and three senior monks carried the precious casket and so, singing antiphons and Kyries, the procession left.

At every stopping-point a cross was incised on a tree; they intended to mark the stations of the journey by erecting crosses at those points later. Miracles of various kinds happened on the way. When they arrived at Pavia they carried the casket into the church of St Michael. Then there were more miracles of the healing of the sick and rumours of the power of Columbanus began to spread.

The Abbot had taken the step of approaching the Archbishop of Milan who promised his help in recovering the monastery's property, but the decisive leadership seems to have been that of the king, who had previously been thought to be rather weak in dealing with his nobles. King Hugh first gathered them in his palace and required them to drink from St Columbanus' cup: the two who refused fled the city, the rest were appropriately awestruck. Then he ordered a public reading of the relevant documents, beginning with the papal bulls, from Pope Honorius onwards, which guaranteed the immunity and freedom of the monastery especially from episcopal interference. Then the king ordered also the reading of the long collection of royal charters, setting out the various donations of property and rights to Bobbio. On the basis of all of this, he ruled in favour of the monastery and against those who had invaded its rights and property. Then the procession went home, accompanied by more miracles on the way. The writer does not tell us how much property was in fact restored. What the story does emphasise is the great reverence for St Columbanus in and around Bobbio, three centuries after his death.

So his remains were replaced safely in the tomb, never to be disturbed again. A great feast of St Columbanus was held. That is the end of the book *Miracula Sancti Columbani* and it is a fitting end to our story also.

Afterword

At the end of a book like this it is natural to ask: how great and lasting was Columbanus' influence? What was his legacy?

We should be careful not to claim too much for him. As explained in ch 11, the great spread of 'Columbanian monasticism' after his death was the work of his Frankish disciples. He himself founded just five monasteries: the three in the Vosges mountains in Francia, one at his temporary stopping place at Bregenz if that may be counted, and one at Bobbio in North Italy. In two ways he was fortunate in his work among the Franks: first, in the sheer quality of his disciples who were people of substance and determination, and secondly, in the fact that social changes meant that such people were rising to power and possessions, and needed also a spiritual vision, just at the time when he could offer it.

Nor must we speak of Columbanus as if his was the only Irish input working in Gaul at the time. The ideal of *peregrinatio* had called a large number of Irish monks, many of whom must remain totally unknown to history while others make a brief appearance in it, such as the three Irish monks mentioned in the Anglo-Saxon Chronicle who arrived in a boat on the coast of Cornwall, and explained to the enquirers of Wessex that they were on pilgrimage for the love of God, but did not know where they would be led. But there were other Irish monks in Gaul who had both a life-story and an influence. Of these the best known is Fursa (or Fursey) who found his way into the pages of Bede's *Ecclesiastical History*. He was an Irish nobleman, called to ascetic and monastic living in Ireland and the recipient of visions about the afterlife, who then settled for a while in East Anglia where he founded a monastery and finally moved to Gaul to do the same. After his death his patron, the Frankish nobleman Eorcenwold, build a shrine and monastery at Peronne, which in time became known as Peronne of the Irish.

Fursa's brother Foillan also came abroad as a pilgrim, was martyred and buried at Fosses, which in time also became a 'monastery of the Irish'. Other Irishmen can be named, such as Kilian and Romanus, who worked as monks and missionaries. All these were quite unconnected with Columbanus; it was a similar situation in England where Irish monks worked among the Anglo-Saxons, in addition to but quite independent of Aidan and his team on Lindisfarne.

Nor must we exaggerate his contribution to monasticism. He did not bring monasticism to Gaul; it had flourished in the cities of the south long before his arrival and continued to flourish there during his lifetime and beyond. His role was to introduce a somewhat different form of monasticism and to establish it in the countryside, as distinct from the cities, and in the north of the country as distinct from the south.

But the stories about him show him to be a man of considerable impact, and this we do not play down. Those who met and responded to him, or responded to his charisma mediated through others, found their lives changed. His was an intriguing and wide-ranging personality, sometime totally implacable, sometimes capable of great gentleness and concern for others.

All this we might know if we simply had his *Vita* and the record of his disciple's achievements. But we also have his writings, and these are what make him 'special'. He is the earliest Irish Christian writer known to us; his astonishing competence in Latin makes us look with some awe at the early Irish monasteries and their schools; it is through him, through his monastic rules and sermons, that we can sense the almost unbelievable single-mindedness and toughness of the earliest Irish Christian style. It is through his letters that we can see something of the bafflement, of the struggling with reality, that was part of his coming to terms with the Christian life of Europe which inevitably he saw as something soft and decadent.

His *Vita* in many ways shows the conventions of hagiography. But in his writings he can speak even to modern people. Not that we can imitate; we must live in our own century; but we can be jolted by him into questioning both his and our own Christian principles and foundations, so that our commitment may be made with more thought and conviction.

For Further Reading

The only complete edition of Columbanus' writings (but not including *Precamur Patrem*) is *Sancti Columbani Opera*, edited by G. S. M. Walker, published by the Dublin Institute for Advanced Studies, 1970. This is a scholarly edition with Latin text, English translation, Introduction and notes. A small book, *Columbanus in His Own Words*, by Tomás Ó Fiaich, was published by Veritas Publications in 1974 and contains a number of extracts.

There is no English translation of the whole of Jonas' *Vita*. An English version of Book I was reprinted by Llanerch Publishers in 1993. A French translation of both books, *Vie de Saint Colomban et de ses Disciples*, translated by Adalbert de Vogüé with introduction and notes, was published by Abbaye de Bellefontaine in 1988.

Readers who would like to follow the saint's journey across Europe will enjoy *The Eagle and the Dove*, by Katharine Lack, SPCK Triangle 2000. Those who would like to follow discussion about the authenticity of his works should consult *Columbanus: Studies on the Latin Writings*, ed M. Lapidge, the Boydell Press, 1997.

Many of the standard histories contain chapters or sections on Columbanus. Particularly useful are *Early Christian Ireland*, by T. M. Charles-Edwards (Cambridge University Press 2000); *Ireland and her Neighbours in the Seventh Century* by Michael Richter (Four Courts Press 1999); *The Merovingian Kingdoms 450-751* by Ian Wood (Longman Group UK 1994).

For the last chapter Michael Richter's book *Bobbio in the Early Middle Ages* (Four Courts Press 2008) is essential and contains fascinating documentary evidence for the position he maintains.

Index